The Stardust Road

&

Sometimes I Wonder

The Stardust Road

&

Sometimes I Wonder

The Autobiography
of Hoagy Carmichael

by Hoagy Carmichael

New introduction and select discography
by John Edward Hasse

Sometimes I Wonder

cowritten with
Stephen Longstreet

DA CAPO PRESS

Library of Congress Cataloging-in-Publication Data

Carmichael, Hoagy, 1899–
  [Stardust road]
  The stardust road & Sometimes I wonder: the autobiographies of Hoagy
Carmichael / by Hoagy Carmichael; new introduction and select discography
by John Edward Hasse; Sometimes I wonder cowritten with Stephen Longstreet.
     p.   cm.
  Reprint: Originally published: New York: Rinehart & Co. (Stardust road),
1946; and Farrar, Straus & Giroux (Sometimes I wonder), 1965.
  ISBN 0-306-80899-4 (alk. paper)
  1. Carmichael, Hoagy, 1899– . 2. Composers–United States–Biography. I.
Hasse, John Edward, 1948– . II. Longstreet, Stephen, 1907– . III. Carmichael,
Hoagy, 1899– . Sometimes I wonder. IV. Title. V. Title: Stardust road. VI.
Title: Sometimes I wonder.
ML410.C327A3   1999
782.42164′ 092–dc21   98-46948
[b]   CIP
                                                                             MN

First Da Capo Press edition 1999

This Da Capo Press paperback edition of *The Stardust Road & Sometimes I Wonder*
consists of an unabridged republication of *The Stardust Road*, first published in
New York in 1946, reprinted here by arrangement with Hoagy Bix Carmichael,
Executor of the Estate of Hoagy Carmichael, and of *Sometimes I Wonder*, first
published in New York in 1965, reprinted here by arrangement with Farrar,
Straus & Giroux, Inc. It is supplemented by a new introduction and select discography by John Edward Hasse.

Published by Da Capo Press, Inc.
A Member of Perseus Books Group

INTRODUCTION

Hoagy Carmichael was a true American original. First of all, there was his name, so unique that he became one of those few public figures—along with Cole, Eubie, and Elvis—that you could identify by his first name alone.

Then there was that singing voice—the flat, Hoosier cadences—and that laconic public persona, impossible to mistake for anyone else's. And there was his unusual career path—from law student, lawyer, and Wall Street employee to hit songwriter and celebrity via records, motion pictures, radio, and television.

But most original of all were the songs Carmichael wrote, songs that typically sound like nobody else's.

Hoagland Howard Carmichael was born in Bloomington, Indiana on November 22, 1899, the oldest child of Howard and Lida Carmichael. His father made a fitful living as a horse-and-buggy operator, later as an electrician; his mother played piano to accompany silent movies and to entertain students at Indiana University fraternity dances. The family teetered at the edge of poverty, but Carmichael had a happy childhood. As a boy, he thrilled to the music of the visiting circuses, and absorbed the music of the nearby black churches. And there was the newfangled ragtime his mother played, rocking the piano as she beat out the raggedy rhythms of Scott Joplin's *Maple Leaf Rag* and other toe-tapping pieces.

During his teenaged years Carmichael's family moved fifty miles northeast to Indianapolis, and there Hoagy came under the spell of an African-American pianist named Reggie DuValle, who played ragtime and the hot rhythms of the incoming jazz music, and who gave Carmichael a great piece of advice. "Never play anything that ain't *right*," he said. "You may not make a lot of money, but you'll never get hostile with yourself."

Back in Bloomington to attend Indiana University, Carmichael seemingly majored in campus capers, girls, and hot music. In *The Stardust Road* he fondly recounts the antics of his crowd. His band, Carmichael's Collegians, earned a following on campus, then a reputation in the region, traveling in Indiana and Ohio to perform for young people. It was the 1920s, and young people were flocking to dance halls to dance to the new jazz. If, for many black innovators and followers, jazz represented a forward-looking action, for many whites, it represented a *re*action, part of the youthful social upheaval in the years after World War I that led many young people to rebel against the social mores of their parents.

If the piano playing of his mother and of Reggie DuValle had exerted the greatest musical influence on Carmichael's first two decades, he profoundly experienced the power of two innovative jazz cornetists: one, Bix Beiderbecke, white, Northern, and dramatically short-lived; the other, Louis Armstrong, black, Southern, and long-lived.

Leon "Bix" Beiderbecke, from Davenport, Iowa, was earning a reputation playing dates in the Midwest when Carmichael encountered him. They met at a dance in Bloomington and became fast friends. As Carmichael recalled in *The Stardust Road*, he was knocked out by Beiderbecke's sound.

> Bix played four notes and that wound up the afternoon party. The notes were beautiful, and perfectly timed. The notes weren't blown—they were hit, like a mallet hits a chime, and his tone had a richness that can only come from the heart. I rose violently from the piano bench and fell, exhausted, onto a davenport. He had completely ruined me. That sounds idiotic, but it is the truth.

For Beiderbecke and his band, The Wolverines, Carmichael wrote his first surviving piece: the composer called it "Free Wheeling," but when the record came out, it had a new title, *Riverboat Shuffle*.

Cornetist Louis Armstrong had moved from New Orleans to Chicago in 1922 to join his mentor, Joe "King" Oliver, and soon Armstrong's reputation would eclipse that of Oliver. In about 1923, Carmichael and some friends went to Chicago and heard Armstrong playing with Oliver. "Louis Armstrong's latest record releases, with the beautiful trumpet passages and the gut-bucket vocals," recalled Carmichael in *The Stardust Road*, "kept our hearts pounding."

Carmichael completed his bachelor's degree in 1925 and a law degree in 1926. By this time, though, music was pulling at him more strongly than ever. A brief stint practicing law in West Palm Beach, Florida was interrupted when the force of his creativity propelled him inexorably towards a career in show business. He had made his first recordings as a bandleader and his compositions were beginning to be published in New York. When he happened upon a recording of his composition of "Washboard Blues" performed by Red Nichols, he was so impressed that he abandoned law forever in favor of music.

Not long after Mills Music Company of New York City published Carmichael's song *Stardust*, he heeded Gotham's siren song—as so many other young and ambitious people have before and since—and moved there to make it in show business. There, in the jazz capital of the world, he met and recorded with some of the best and brightest stars in the jazz firmament—Henry "Red" Allen, Louis Armstrong, Mildred Bailey, Benny Goodman, Eddie Lang, Glenn Miller, and Jack Teagarden. Carmichael lined up bands of leading jazzmen to record his songs—*Rockin' Chair*, *Georgia on My Mind*, and *Lazy River*, all in 1930. In a five-year stretch from 1929 to 1934, Carmichael, as bandleader, made 36 recordings for Victor. In 1931, the American Society of Composers, Authors, and Publishers (ASCAP) admitted him to membership, signifying his arrival in the songwriting fraternity.

Carmichael teamed up with a younger songwriter, lyricist Johnny Mercer from Savannah, Georgia, and their *Lazybones* of 1933 became a huge hit. They would write together on and off for several decades, producing 36 collaborations. The gifted, versatile Mercer, with his rich ear for the American vernacular, would became Carmichael's best songwriting partner.

In 1931 Beiderbecke died. His death closed a large chapter in Carmichael's life. He deeply missed Beiderbecke's friendship and the inspiration of his playing. Carmichael now seemed to want the good life more than the jazz life, the widest audience more than the hippest audience. Perhaps influenced by the example of his friend George Gershwin, Carmichael moved in 1936 to Hollywood, where, as he put it, "the rainbow hits the ground for composers." In 1937 he joined Paramount Pictures as a staff songwriter, and collaborated with Frank Loesser on such songs as *Two Sleepy People*, *Small Fry*, and that perennial favorite of piano-playing kids, *Heart and Soul*. In 1937 he also landed his first role as a movie actor, a small part as a piano player in *Topper*.

By now Carmichael was a husband; in 1936 he had married Ruth Meinardi of Winona Lake, Indiana. The couple would have two sons—Hoagy Bix and Randy Bob. Besides writing songs for the movies and, with Johnny Mercer, a failed Broadway musical—*I Walk with Music* (1939)—Carmichael continued to write independent songs for Tin Pan Alley: *Baltimore Oriole*, *I Get Along without You Very Well*, and *Skylark*.

Carmichael achieved his greatest celebrity in the 1940s: recording for Decca Records; acting in movies such as *To Have and Have Not* (1944, featuring, as one wag has put it, "Hoagy, Bogey, and Bacall"), *The Best Years of Our Lives* (1946), and *Young Man with a Horn* (1950); and hosting his own radio series for the NBC, CBS, and Mutual Radio networks. In 1946 his first book of memoirs, *The Stardust Road*, was published. Carmichael was now at the peak of his popularity; his songs had become, as one British observer put it, "the virtual accompaniment to daily living."

In 1948 he made a successful debut in British variety at the London Casino, and in 1951 he played two weeks at the London Palladium. As he had deftly adapted to new communications media in the past, in the 1950s, Carmichael moved rather easily into television, hosting a 1953 variety program, *The Saturday Night Revue*, and in

1959–'60 appearing in a straight dramatic role as Jonesy, the hired ranchhand, on the Western series *Laramie*.

In 1951 his collaboration with Johnny Mercer, *In the Cool, Cool, Cool of the Evening*, an ebullient song anticipating a party, earned its songwriters an Academy Award for best Motion Picture Song. Carmichael continued to write songs, such as *My Resistance Is Low* and *Winter Moon*, but as rock 'n' roll took center stage musically, he found it increasingly difficult to get his songs published and recorded. And in 1955, his marriage ended. Yet, a number of his old songs found new favor, as when Ray Charles transformed *Georgia on My Mind* into rhythm & blues, creating a huge hit and earning Charles a Grammy Award.

In his classic and authoritative book, *American Popular Song*, Alec Wilder called Carmichael "the most talented, inventive, sophisticated, and jazz-oriented of all the great craftsmen" (Wilder's term for the songwriters who worked outside of musical theater) and ranked him just below the likes of George Gershwin, Cole Porter, and Jerome Kern. But Wilder may have underestimated Carmichael's place by focusing on musical-theater songwriters, thus undervaluing the strength and durability of songs—such as Carmichael's—which work as stand-alones, independent of any theatrical production. And by ranking Carmichael below Gershwin and Kern, Wilder may have been comparing oranges and apples.

All of the great musical theater songwriters lived and worked in New York City, and wrote from the urban, consciously sophisticated perspective of twentieth century Manhattan. Carmichael's songs, on the other hand, drew at least as much inspiration from the music of his native Indiana and from the jazz of New Orleans and Chicago as from the Tin

Pan Alley songwriting tradition of New York City. In his songs, whether the lyrics were written by a partner or by himself (for instance, *Lazy River* and *Rockin' Chair*), Carmichael frequently celebrated a simpler time and place, offering us what Larry Hart called "a dreamlike vision of the wholeness of rural and small-town life." The twentieth century intrudes little into the sensibility of Carmichael's songs.

Carmichael had a relaxed and informal approach to melody. His best songs—*Stardust* and *Skylark*—sound as if he magically captured elegant improvisations in mid-air and pasted them onto sheet music. His style as a songwriter and singer-pianist was sincere, charming, folksy, and laid-back. Indeed, almost unique among songwriters, he is known primarily for his ballads.

One of his ballads, *Stardust*, became an extraordinary success, an evergreen among musicians and audiences, and an American icon, haunting the collective consciousness with its longing for lost love, its images of purple dusk and climbing stars, and its indelible, poignant melody. With at least 1,300 recorded versions worldwide, *Stardust* ranks as one of the most recorded songs in history, possibly *the* most recorded. It has joined other songs of his—*Georgia on My Mind, Lazy River, Skylark, Rockin' Chair, The Nearness of You*—as staples and standards of the repertories of jazz and popular-song, at least as durable as great public buildings of the period.

But what of his two memoirs? The first, *The Stardust Road*, was published in 1946, but, oddly, its narrative ends in about 1931. *The Stardust Road* is not so much an autobiography as a series of personal reminiscences, many of them vivid, some sentimental, and a few poetic. Carmichael writes in a highly personal style that mixes memories, surrealist fantasy, humor, and even fictional techniques. The book covers the period from his childhood to 1931, when his close friend and hero Beiderbecke died. It evokes a time and place when hot jazz had captivated many young Americans, when Beiderbecke and Armstrong were cultural heroes, when the new jazz music found a legion of fans at colleges, when musical parodies were a fad among young people. Carmichael's playfulness and inventiveness, his intense feelings for the hot music, his close friendship with Beiderbecke, and his nostalgic yearning for life in small-town Indiana are recurring themes.

Although the narrative moves generally forward in time, there are flashbacks, forward leaps, asides, and brief, almost improvised, flashes of reminiscence. Indeed, one might call the pulse syncopated, for in its pace as well as in its romantic and poetic aspects, the book conjures up the hot jazz and dance music that Carmichael loved deeply.

The book evidently was completed in 1933, for in an unpublished letter Carmichael mentions completing *Lazy Bones* and *Old Man Harlem* (both issued in 1933) and notes that "I have been spending a year writing a book. Just finished it." Why the book did not appear for another thirteen years is unexplained; perhaps during the Great Depression no publisher could be found. By the end of World War II, however, Carmichael was a much greater celebrity—in fact, because of his many hit songs and motion picture appearances, his was by then a household name.

The Stardust Road concludes with a long letter to the composer from his friend Howard "Wad" Allen, which breezily covers events from 1931 to 1946.

One of the recurrent motifs in *The Stardust Road* is of young people's involvement with the new jazz music. For Carmichael and his gang, jazz symbolized a reaction against the restrictions and conventions of the older generation, against the conformity of middle-class society. In *The Stardust Road* Carmichael created an evocative memoir of his youth and early career, of the siren song of hot jazz, of the white jazz scene in the Midwest of the 1920s, of the brilliant music and sad demise of Bix Beiderbecke.

Judging from the writing style in Carmichael's second book, *Sometimes I Wonder,* it was heavily "ghosted" by Stephen Longstreet, the versatile visual artist who illustrated, wrote, or edited dozens of books, among them, several on New Orleans jazz: *The Real Jazz Old and New* (1956) and *Sportin' House: A History of the New Orleans Sinners and the Birth of Jazz* (1965). *Sometimes I Wonder* re-covers some of the same ground as Carmichael's earlier volume, but extends the story by twenty-some years, into the 1950s. Here we meet the personalities from jazz, popular song, and the film world with whom Carmichael worked—for example, Johnny Mercer and Bob Hope—but most of the emphasis is on Carmichael himself.

The first book offers an individual, natural, and vivid writing style; the second covers far more of Carmichael's life and, with the chronological framework that Longstreet no doubt introduced, provides a more coherent personal history.

Carmichael's narrative in *Sometimes I Wonder* ends by the late 1950s. What of his story after that period?

He lived out his final years in Rancho Mirage, California on the edge of a golf course. In 1977, Carmichael married the actress Dorothy Wanda McKay after what was termed "a long courtship." Golfing and coin collecting were two favorite pastimes, and he was no doubt delighted to see his royalties grow as songs he contributed to the standard repertory continued to be recorded by a wide variety of artists, ranging from jazz and pop musicians to country singers and rock bands. Carmichael continued to write songs, but the music business showed little interest in them. He did manage, in 1957, to publish a collection of songs for children: *Hoagy Carmichael's Music Shop.*

Increasing honors and recognitions marked the last decade of his life. In 1971 the Songwriters Hall of Fame selected him as one of its ten initial inductees, and the following year, Indiana University awarded him an honorary doctorate. In 1974 Indiana University's Lilly Library, a leading rare-book collection, mounted an exhibition devoted to Carmichael, replete with an exhibition catalog. In 1979 Carnegie Hall hosted a tribute, "The Star Dust Road: A Hoagy Carmichael Jubilee." The following year, the Book-of-the-Month Club issued a four-LP anthology, *Hoagy Carmichael, From "Star Dust" to "Ole Buttermilk Sky."* A British playwright, Adrian Mitchell, wrote a stage production, *Hoagy, Bix, and Wolfgang Beethoven Bunkhaus*, that, after playing at London's King's Head Theater, moved in 1980 to the United States, playing at Indianapolis's Indiana Repertory Theater and Los Angeles's Mark Taper Forum.

After suffering a heart attack, Carmichael died on December 27, 1981, and was returned to his native Bloomington for burial on January 4, 1982. In the years since his death Carmichael's star has kept rising as the elevation and celebration of his life and legacy continued. In 1983 a songbook of his work was issued, *Hoagy Carmichael: The Stardust Melodies of . . . .* In 1986 the Carmichael family donated his archives, piano, and memorabilia to Indiana University, which established a Hoagy Carmichael Collection in its Archives of Traditional Music and the Hoagy Carmichael Room to permanently display selections from the collection. Hidden away in the papers are numerous nuggets for researchers to mine, including interviews, radio programs, and even drawings for devices that Carmichael sought to patent, such as a Rube Goldberg–like machine that would break open an egg, stir, cook, and scramble it. Such finds show that Carmichael's inventiveness was not confined to music.

Culminating a ten-year research project by this author, in 1988 the Indiana Historical Society and Smithsonian Recordings jointly issued a four-LP anthology, *The Classic Hoagy Carmichael*, based on auditioning 3,000 recordings of songs composed by Carmichael to select the final 57. The album was nominated for two Grammy Awards in the categories of "Best Historical Album" and "Best Album Notes." In the 1990s record companies issued or re-issued a half-dozen CD anthologies of recordings of his songs.

And now, in the year of Carmichael's centennial, comes this combined reissue of his two memoirs—a welcome way indeed to remember and appreciate this singular American talent.

JOHN EDWARD HASSE
Alexandria, Virginia
December 1998

JOHN EDWARD HASSE is Curator of American Music at the Smithsonian Institution's National Museum of American History in Washington, DC. While pursuing his Ph.D. degree at Indiana University, he conceived of, and began researching, a boxed set of recordings, *The Classic Hoagy Carmichael*, for which he served as producer and author of the accompanying booklet. Hasse is the author of *Beyond Category: The Life and Genius of Duke Ellington* (available from Da Capo Press). He also serves as a commentator for National Public Radio and lectures widely on the arts and American music.

SELECT DISCOGRAPHY
compiled by John Edward Hasse

Carmichael the Songwriter

McKenna, Dave. *A Celebration of Hoagy Carmichael*. Concord Jazz.

Various artists. *The Classic Hoagy Carmichael*. Three discs, boxed, with a 64-page booklet written by John Edward Hasse. Smithsonian Recordings and Indiana Historical Society. Includes 57 recordings, spanning the years 1928–1988, by Louis Armstrong, Hoagy Carmichael, Benny Goodman, Ethel Waters, Mildred Bailey, Frank Sinatra, Jo Stafford, Ella Fitzgerald, Sarah Vaughn, Mel Tormé, Ray Charles, Wynton Marsalis, and others. Available from the Indiana Historical Society, 315 West Ohio Street, Indianapolis, IN 46202. Telephone 1-800-447-1830.

_____. *A Hoagy Carmichael Songbook*. Concord Special Products. Includes Rosemary Clooney, Ruby Braff, Dave McKenna, and Mel Tormé.

_____. *Hoagy Carmichael Songbook*. BMG. Includes Helen Ward, Kate Smith, Phil Harris, Kay Star, Louis Prima, Tommy Dorsey, and Glenn Miller.

_____. *Hoagy Carmichael*. (American Songbook Series.) Smithsonian Collection of Recordings. Includes Frank Sinatra, Mildred Bailey, Billy Eckstine, Johnny Mercer, Carmen McRae, and Tony Bennett.

_____. *The Song Is...Hoagy Carmichael*. ASV Living Era. Recordings from 1929–'39 and broadcasts from 1938–'46, featuring Louis Armstrong, Nat Gonella, the Mills Brothers, and Chick Webb

_____. *Stardust: Capitol Sings Hoagy Carmichael*. Capitol. Includes Nat "King" Cole, Johnny Mercer, Kay Starr, and the Four Freshmen.

_____. *Stardust: The Jazz Giants Play Hoagy Carmichael*. Prestige. Includes Art Tatum, Ben Webster, Dave Brubeck, and John Coltrane.

Wilber, Bob. *The Music of Hoagy Carmichael as Conceived and Arranged by Bob Wilber*. Audiophile. Features Maxine Sullivan (vocal) on five selections.

Carmichael the Recording Artist

Carmichael, Hoagy. *Hoagy Carmichael, Volume One.* JSP.

_____. *Hoagy Carmichael, Volume Two.* JSP.

_____. *Hong Kong Blues.* MCA Special Products.

_____. Stardust, and Much More. BMG.

_____. V-Disc Recordings. Collector's Choice Music.

the
stardust
road

hoagy
carmichael

PART ONE

While I am indebted to a large number of people for certain facts and anecdotes contained herein, I am particularly indebted to Wad Allen and Harry Hostetter and to the Beiderbecke and Moenkhaus families for their wholehearted co-operation and assistance.

Since the contents of this book are factual, it should be plain to the reader that the late Bix Beiderbecke and the late William Moenkhaus had a decided influence on my early life. It is the wonderful memories of my association with these two talented personalities that prompted the writing of the book and, so, to their memory I dedicate it.

The phone rang and I picked it up. It was Wad Allen. "Bix died," he said.

Wad laughed a funny laugh. I laughed too. "Company for Monk," I said.

"I wonder if it will hurt old Gabriel's feelings to play second trumpet?" Wad asked.

I sat there and the open wire buzzed in my ear. I could hear Wad's breathing, then suddenly, but gradually getting clearer, I heard something else.

"I can hear him," I said. "I can hear him fine from here."

Over and around the sound I heard Wad's voice.

"Sure," he said shakily. "So can I."

"I guess he didn't die, then."

"I'm glad to hear that," Wad said. "It was in Winchell's column, just a squib, but I'm glad he didn't die."

"Do you remember how Monk used to say *he* was going to die any day now?" I asked, and I was laughing.

"Yeah," Wad said. "He died all right. Died to keep from paying me that three bucks he owed me."

"Not Bix . . ."

"No, Monk. Monk didn't die last winter. Bix didn't die last night."

"I'm glad to know that," I said. "I can hear them both fine from where I am."

"They're coming in better for me, too," Wad said. "I just saw a cow go by—one by one," he added, quoting Monk.

"Call me up again," I told him, "when somebody else doesn't die."

But Wad had hung up. I tilted back in the chair before my desk and felt tears behind my eyes. So I laughed again—and then I let go of my mind and it moved away, back to 1924.

I was on the lawn of the Pi Phi house at Indiana University doing a jig and I saw in the gloom another gyrating figure. It was Harry Hostetter.

Harry was a town boy whom I had known since the days of kid football, and he was a fellow who watched and encouraged me during my early days as a pianist. But he had been away, doing a hitch in the Navy; now he seemed to be back and afflicted with St. Vitus's dance on the Pi Phi lawn.

It was a midnight serenade in Sorority Row by an orchestra huddled in the back of a two-ton truck. Light cut dimly across a weird assortment of enchanted listeners as a cornet carved passages of heat and beauty in the night.

"That's the Wolverines," I yelled. "How's that for a band?"

But Harry didn't answer me except with moans of delight.

Farewell Blues came to a stop and Harry and I stood

there a moment not saying anything, for there was nothing for us to say. Then Harry rubbed his hands through his hair as though he was just awaking and looked at me and smiled.

"Hello, Hoagy," he said absently.

"Hi, Harry."

Then, earnestly, he said: "I traveled all over the world, Hoagy, and I was homesick all the time. But worse, even worse than that, was something that gnawed at me. Something I couldn't identify until just now."

I realized what he meant, vaguely. He had heard it and he had had it. But I didn't say anything. I just stood there and waited.

"In foreign ports," he went on, "I used to hunt dives in search of music. Sometimes I heard weird stuff that gave me a tingle—a hint of what I wanted to hear—but there was no satisfaction, really, and I thought of you and your bands pretty often and I wondered how you were coming along. I had a craving for American music —dance music . . ."

I started to say something but Harry didn't hear me.

"I hadn't heard any jazz, you know, except for a few records, but these records I heard made me *really* long for home; and when I did get back I heard your band— and it felt awfully good—but it didn't floor me."

"This afternoon . . ." I began again.

"Tonight," Harry ignored me, going on in a deadly serious monotone, "I was walking home from Tom Huff's pool hall about one-thirty and I heard a cornet. It seemed like it was miles away. I couldn't even exactly hear it, but I could feel it. And I knew I had to get where it was. *I* didn't run, but I found my legs running up Third

Street, and as I grew closer I knew I was going to find what I was looking for. My heart was jumping with excitement when my ears were able to catch the complete rhythm and harmony, and when you saw me here tonight, *I was there.* I had come all the way. That cornet and that band took me on a risky ride to paradise. If it had let me down on just one note it would have wrecked my journey—and," he added perfectly seriously, "perhaps my life."

"He didn't fail you," I said.

Harry shook his head in mute agreement.

"Nor me," I said. "That's Bix Beiderbecke and the band is the Wolverines. I heard Bix once before in Chicago but he didn't have the finish he's got now, and this afternoon, over at the Kappa Sig house, when I suggested they play a tune or two, I got scared. I dreaded to hear Bix play."

"I know," Harry said. "He might not be perfect and he *had* to be perfect."

"That's it. Well, there's George Johnson and Bix and they got Dick Voynow on the piano, Jimmy Hartwell playing clarinet and alto sax, Bob Gillette on the banjo, Min Leibrook on the bass, and Vic Moore beats the drums."

We were still standing out there in the dark and the cold but Harry hadn't moved and he was listening.

"So I suggest we play a tune and I go over to the piano and start chording *Dipper Mouth Blues.* Jimmy Hartwell joins in and starts doodling on his sax and I start tingling. I could feel my hands trying to shake and getting cold when I saw Bix get out his horn. Boy, he took it!"

Harry was watching me and in his face was suppressed excitement.

"Just four notes," I said. "But he didn't blow them —he hit 'em like a mallet hits a chime—and his tone, the richness . . ." I groped for words.

"He was talking to you—oh, more than that. I know what you mean," Harry finished helplessly.

"Whatever it was," I said, "he ruined me. I got up from the piano and staggered over and fell on the davenport."

Harry put out his hand. Solemnly I shook it.

Now these things happened in the spring of the year 1924 and they happened on the campus of Indiana University at Bloomington. It was a town then of some twelve thousand inhabitants and as many maples; situated on a shelf of limestone in part of the state only six miles from Brown County, that picturesque part of Indiana known mainly to us Hoosiers as the home of Kin Hubbard's "Abe Martin," the comic philosopher.

The music that did these things to us was called "*jazz.*" Jazz had been born early in the century, as had we. Jazz was groping its way through the early twenties as we were groping ours.

The first World War had been fought, and in the backwash conventions had tumbled. There was rebellion, then, against the accepted, the proper and the old. Woodrow Wilson had not so long before declared: ". . . that everything for which America had fought had been accomplished. . . ." The shooting war was over but the rebellion was just getting started.

And for us jazz articulated. I was a jazz pianist. "Hot piano," we called it then. I was trying to create jazz. It said what we wanted to say though what that was we might not know.

That's my friend, Bill Moenkhaus, who was looking for a nickel's worth of chicken and his father's remorse. That's my friend Wad Allen that he found.

Monk was the one with the ancient coupe—the coupe with the upholstery that suffered from "chetherweg," a dread disease that causes a slightly nervous lifting of the forefinger, and, in its latter stages, is given to causing its victim to snatch up a telephone and scream: "I don't remember you, but I remember your father."

Wad Allen was the one that lent Monk the three dollars. The three dollars to help cover a bad check with which Monk had bought the coupe in Indianapolis.

"The lights went out," Monk explained with desperate insincerity, "and I had to hire a little Negro boy to carry a lantern in front of me for miles. He absorbed all my ready capital." Monk was sunk.

Monk's despondency had now reached such depths that he was muttering incoherent things in broken German. This delighted Wad so that he lent him the three dollars. Soon they were hissing silly sounds at each other and found that it was soothing to the soul.

Life had been boring a moment before, but now it was much better. They walked toward the campus, throwing their tongues out at each other like a snake. They ran part way down Fifth Street and as they approached the intersection of Indiana Avenue, where the library stands, they were screaming such things as "hydrant!" "faucet!" and "lukewarm!" or "buskirk!" They laughed not together, but at each other. Monk's laugh was like the wail of a dying coyote and this was a new sensation to Wad. Finally they grew weak and sat on the ground moaning "three dollars."

Now this may seem an amateurish exhibition of foolishness. Nevertheless, to these two it was a means of escape from boredom. Maybe it was the expression of jazz in the spiritual sense. Monk, practically an unknown on the campus at this point, began to write.

And this is the Wad Allen who had arrived in Bloomington to attend Indiana University in the fall of 1921. Wad brought with him an abundance of self-confidence, a cheap violin, the praises of his parents and the prayers of his music tutor.

Four years later I received the same violin, express collect, from the most northern reaches of Michigan. It wasn't recognizable as a musical instrument, but the note that came with it cleared up the mystery.

> The violin has served us well as a snow shovel but you, Hogwash McGorkle, shall have the sad remains in memory of its dead father, an old man from Detroit.
> (Signed) Wad and Monk
> (Violin Benders)

The violin had done well enough by Wad his first year in the university and had enabled him to make twelve dollars a week playing picture-show music. But Wad's roommate bought a saxophone on which he was given to slap-tonguing arpeggios. Wad heard the siren call and his own artistic aspirations as a concert violinist withered away. He, too, bought a saxophone.

Monk was a professor's son, who had made several

trips to Switzerland and Germany. He walked with a slight limp, and according to Monk this was the result of an accident he suffered while climbing the Matterhorn. A lie of course, but we enjoyed believing it. His face was big and bony out of which stared watery gray eyes and the long hands that dangled at his sides wore blue fingernails. He made straight "A's" in a bored sort of way and as his writings progressed became the founder and chief spokesman of a campus cult which he named the Bent Eagles. Through his surrealistic nonsensical writings he became a campus character in the eyes of most people and a fabulous literary figure in the minds of a few.

Monk had other accomplishments. He could put an eight ball into the side pocket with skill and his choice of invectives thrown at the balls that failed to drop were masterpieces. But more important, Monk had studied classical music both at home and abroad and his talents at piano and cello were applauded at faculty functions, high-school recitals and some times by his college fraternity brothers, the Phi Gams. But these instruments were destined to be neglected in favor of a bass horn when the roots of jazz took hold in Bloomington. Why he never played in my orchestras I can't quite recall except that maybe I couldn't stand to watch him blow the thing.

I remember other very early days in Bloomington. I remember running my hand through my hair, and in a pattern of confusion, my mother picking "bugs" from that hair. I had got the "bugs" from the boy who sat next to me and I was in the second grade or perhaps it was the third.

"Hoagland!" I can hear her exclaim. "Just look at your hair!"

I was cheerfully imperturbed. "What's the matter?"

"Bugs, Hoagland. Nice people don't have bugs in their hair."

My mother always calls me Hoagland. And the Hoagland memories are of solid things, warm and endearing things. Hoagland—a boy with dusty feet coming into the cold parlor where stood the upright golden oak piano. Outside life moved on the quiet tree-lined street, but it moved at a modest tempo.

I don't want to forget Hoagland memories. Other people call me Hoagy, but it is Hoagland that remembers the long chromatic runs my mother played when the redskins bit the dust on the flickering silver screen. My mother played the picture-show music and I got in free. Hoagy, the most important kid in town, gets in the picture show free because his mother plays the music. Everybody calls me Hoagy except my mother and my grandparents. I don't want to forget the Hoagland memories.

I was born in Bloomington at the turn of the century and they tell me that my Grandma Robison spent many a weary hour rubbing my head into a normal shape. I grew into a normal boy, a member of the East Side gang which in the days of screaming youth knew no distinction between blacks and whites. Bucktown, where the Negroes lived, was only a few blocks away.

Monk was born in Bloomington and he too was a normal boy. Somewhat brighter than most of us though, and since he was a member of the faculty gang, we seldom rubbed elbows on Dunn Meadow.

Dunn Meadow is where the circuses pitched their

big tents; where we played baseball and football. You could cross the streets of Bloomington alone in those days, you didn't need a cop to stop the traffic, and you could race to Dunn Meadow and there would be big kids there playing baseball and they'd let you play because they didn't have enough to make two teams. North of the meadow where the cows roamed, the tall iron weeds made wonderful tepees when cut and stacked in the right manner. No good in the rain though.

It did rain, and the baseball game was called off. I was blue and mad. I came home disconsolate and wandered into the icy parlor and banged on the old upright with my fists. And then, through the dripping maples, I heard Mr. Foley tolling *Indiana Franjipani* on the student tower bells. I remember each separate note as it came winging through the rain. When Mr. Foley had finished I went over to the piano and with one finger started picking out the notes. And suddenly I was amazed. I was picking them out correctly. I hadn't thought about doing it but I had done it.

The Dunn Meadow Demons lost an incompetent sixty-pound third baseman that day. Baseball was gone. The piano had me.

Once, before that, when I was only four years old my family moved to Indianapolis and we lived on Lockerbie Street for a while. And I remember riding on the shoulder of a man who'd take me to the corner and buy me candy. When we were together and the fire engines went by (headquarters was in the neighborhood) he would count them for me. Always there were fifty fire engines carefully counted by James Whitcomb Riley as I sat on his shoulder. Always fifty.

It was during that period in Indianapolis that my Grandmother Robison came from Bloomington once to visit us, bringing boxes of fruit to add to our meager larder. When she departed I staged such a heartrending scene that the engineer held up the train and my dad promised to take us back to Bloomington soon.

I was too young to recognize the feeling for Bloomington that was growing within me. The compulsion to be there, to return there, to take from Bloomington the things it offered. Things I know now were more fundamental than kids and safe streets and broad meadows where you could run and fall panting in the thick cool grass as you gasped "safe." But I felt there were things there that I must have there and always I wanted to go back.

The years have pants! Yon
Helmet of the sunburnt gone
Lingering odors of the dead
Who yesterday the wigwam fed.

'Tis not the grave of Hermann Bort
Who's life was like an ugly wart,
Fold up the trumpet which he drove
And pour the music in the stove:

'Twas his to live and now to die
Who remembers not the pie
That each and every evening went
Into the mouth that now lies bent.

A tear or two, then from us sweep
The memories of men who sleep
Long live the drunken alphabet
The time for us has not come—yet.

Moenkhaus wrote that. A eulogy to a fellow musician who had passed away. I was sitting in the Book Nook with him and he recited it. Back in Bloomington once more, enrolled in the university, sitting in the Book Nook with Moenkhaus. Our pants were long then, and occasionally had money in them. I was trying to interrupt Monk long enough to tell him about a band, Jordan's band, but Monk wouldn't listen and Wad Allen came in then. He didn't listen either because he had a piece of paper in his hand and he wanted to read from it. It was another work from the pen of Monk. Wad read it to us aloud. As he read it we rocked with the silent glee that bound us because we loved each other.

Thanksgiving Comes But Once A Dozen

Scene:

> Somewhere between a large hotel. Perhaps there is a fire. People are snowing themselves under and the heavens are threatened with lard. In the background are firemen selling small pears.

Enter:

> Women's Compound Tonsil Union singing:
> "On glands and wheels the bakers roar,
> As Harper's chickens, four by four,
> Leap across the bathroom floor.
> Amen."

(Cheers by Mrs. Baker)

First W.C.T.U.

> "Friends, cannons and Thursday!"

(Louder cheers by Mrs. Baker who is affectionately called Old Aunt Cancer in her home town of West Hawkins, Nebraska)

Second W.C.T.U.

> "I am from Roaring Pork, Idaho. I favor neither
> beer near the keg, near beer the keg, nor keg
> near beer."

(Old Aunt Cancer loses control and has an attack of
chetherweg)

Third W.C.T.U.

> (Unable to locate mouth and is speechless)

The End

I was high. I walked over to the piano. What I
played we called *The Death of a Hog.* Wad Allen chanted
an impromptu lyric. Monk screamed his delight. The
Greeks who owned the Book Nook hovered unhappily in
the background and curious onlookers straggled out. We
had the place to ourselves and we gave in to the dirge and
to the piano and our own hysterical delight. Finally we
left. I walked, dazed, to the Kappa Sig house, grateful
for that haven, wondering if we were mad. I had been
confident that the Moenkhaus stuff had no real signifi-
cance, but tonight I wasn't so sure. After all, I had been
inspired to compose a screwy dirge, which under normal
conditions would have been an impossibility. I slept fit-
fully in a damp, swayback bed that hadn't seen clean
sheets in weeks.

But in the morning I felt better about it. The sun
was up on schedule and breakfast went along as usual. I
knew that we were still normal boys and that the spasm
of the night before was a healthy thing. It enabled us to
let off steam and at the same time gave us a new means
of self-expression. We were hams and we got a kick out

of watching the effect of our maniacal mannerisms on others. In no time at all college students roamed the campus quoting Monk and trying to imitate his facial expressions. A couple of professors took it seriously and nearly went daffy. We loved it. We were "characters" and we were creating a little legend around ourselves.

The years have pants.

These were the Brooks Brothers pants days. But let's go back to the first long pants days for a moment. Pants that were tailormade for me at the ripe age of fifteen. Right snazzy for a freshman in high school but the super-intendent kicked them and me out of old B.H.S. when I said something to a little girl in braids. Tattletale! Maybe I deserved to lose my happy home and that was what I got. The family moved to Indianapolis and for a long time I was lonely for Bloomington. But in Indianapolis I found Reggie Duval. The bright moments of that cheer-less period were in Reggie's house.

Reggie Duval was high brown, long fingered, white toothed, happy. He had a pretty wife who fed me while I listened to him play the piano.

He was playing professionally in a dive, but he didn't care if God was in His Heaven and all was right with the world or not. He hit keys where they shouldn't quite be hit, but it came out right. He laughed like a hyena on those keys that gleam with their black and white magic. He knew the Congo tricks and he made ragtime sound stilted. With his head hanging to one side, as if overcome with shyness, he'd play. And I would sit there, absorbed, watching the flighty movements of his brown wonderful hands.

He looks at me and I'm small, very thin, white faced, sixteen. I'm tired too, and getting old. I'm working twelve hours a night running a cement mixer, and wishing Reggie and his wife could live at our house; they are so nice.

"What are you doing there?"

"I bring my thumb down, like that," Reggie says. "I dunno, it just makes it . . ."

"You bring your thumb down on the chord right after you've hit it with your right hand."

"Yeah," he grins. "I want that harmony to *holler.*"

"Laugh," I say.

"Look," Reggie says. "I want it so it sounds right to *me*. And that is the way it sounds rightest."

"It's wonderful . . ."

"Naw, but it's *right*. Never play anything that ain't *right*. You may not make any money, but you'll never get hostile with yourself."

I look at him in wonder and wish again with fervency that they could move into our house.

Our house in 1916 is the thin dark side of a double in the West End of Indianapolis. I had started to Manual High School and was filled with rebellion rather than learning. In one course, designed to be practical, they tried to teach me to shingle a house. Hell, I'd already shingled a whole house, singlehanded, for my Grandpa Robison.

So, I had parted from Manual High, neither of us grieving, and I ran a cement mixer. I worked in a slaughterhouse. I sweated and I worked and I was cheerless. The corner drugstore gang looked with disdain upon the overcoat my mother had painstakingly made for me. (Styled after the one in a big downtown window.)

Then came the war. I weighed myself. I studied the requirements and ate bananas and drank water until I fulfilled them. But something had happened en route though I had shunned bathrooms. I didn't weigh enough.

Back to the slaughterhouse, the cement mixer, the friendless days. Periodic fruitless trips to the recruiting office. And then one day I made it. I was in the Army. Hoagland Carmichael, U.S. Army, November 10, 1918. I drilled for an hour in a public school playground. One whole hour. In the Army. I guess our names were not submitted to headquarters because I never heard another word about it.

And all the time I thought of Bloomington. I remembered the boys I knew, the circuses coming to town, and the flour sacks we collected from boardinghouses and sold to the local grocer for a cent each. Remembered the pop stands we built with the money; the quarry holes where we used to swim. I remember the kindly neighbors who suffered us with never a reproachful word, except when we smoked corn silks in their privies or dumped these same little outhouses with a bang! on Halloween.

When Notre Dame played Indiana University in Indianapolis that fall of the Armistice, all my homesick longings were crystallized. And it got worse when the Bloomington High School team came to play that winter in the state basketball tourney. These boys, the team members, it seemed to me, were my sort of people. Why, I remembered that Bobby Marxson, their star forward (nicknamed "Little Lightning"), was no match for either cousin Sammy Dodds or me during grade-school days. But here he is on top and here am I running a cement mixer.

And so, with ten dollars painfully scraped together, in January, 1919, I went back to Bloomington to re-enter high school. It was a difficult and painful decision. I was old; older than my classmates would be. It would be tough.

But the breaks came my way. Grandma Robison gave me a room and my breakfast. The good smell of the kitchen, of Grandpa's clean workshirt and the bacon gravy that he made himself started each day right.

Hank Wells playing a hot fiddle in the Crescent Theatre pit *ended* each day right. It was Hube Hanna's ten-foot orchestra. What other town but Bloomington would have a five-piece band with a two-reel movie?

Hank played the first hot fiddle I ever heard, maybe the first hot fiddle *ever* heard. Joe Venuti became famous sawing it off hot and lowdown, but perhaps Hank did it first. He played a lot of piano too, and he and Reggie Duval helped me gain my first conception of harmony and jazz.

The Crescent Theatre also held romance. Diluted perhaps by the object of your affections being two rows away, but she was there, under the same roof, seeing the same shifting scenes, listening to the same music.

She is a little on the unobtainable side, being a university campus queen named Kate Cameron; a prom trotter of fame, and doubtless not throbbing with yearning toward a skinny hundred-pounder trying to re-enter high school. But, she sits in the same show and even cats can look at queens though perhaps cats don't get the same reaction.

The movies were exciting and Hube's orchestra in the pit to boot kept us in constant turmoil, ever expectant of the moment when Hube would let go a gob of tobacco juice into the open piano—a signal for fast business with his right hand.

Hank was three years my senior and a Scotsman of the deepest dye. With the cry of "Let's have a coke," someone was sure to say, "I'll buy Hank's." Well, why not? Hank was the center of attraction. He played long and hard at the piano, and if he had the desire to visit his Beta fraternity rooms, the gang usually followed. Gump Carter was always on hand, padding along with his feet at fifty-five degrees, his mouth screwed into a nervous distortion at the anticipation of hearing Hank do *Poor Pauline* again. Gump had suffered a bad case of scarlet fever at the age of six years and rumor had it that he lost considerably more than his hair. Everyone knew Gump, and the Sunday gatherings were not complete without him. Perhaps he organized more jam sessions than anyone else I know.

Gump's weakness was Kate, and he had a tough time keeping track of her whereabouts, in spite of his remarkable ability to show up in three places at once. "Have you seen Kate?" soon became an expression among the boys, meaning everything from "how are you?" to "go to hell."

From the Beta rooms we went to the Candy Kitchen, on the square; in the absence of a piano, someone generally had a nickel handy to start the music box. In the din of this claptrap, all heads were pointed over a table top to take in the latest dirty story picked up from a drummer in the Globe Clothing Store. So that no stone was left unturned, we usually ended up in the new Kappa Alpha Phi rooms above Neeld's Hardware Store to find a game of five hundred in full swing or Ed East teaching the boys the new Kappa song he had written.

Parodies were in vogue. Often, as I hung over the piano to catch the lyric of some song Hank was delivering in his inimitable style, I had my ears burned.

> Underneath the sheltering palms,
> Oh, honey, wait for me.

Sunday nights found us behind the Observatory shooting dice or in the Kappa rooms until the early hours of the morning, playing cards and arguing about women. Then home to bed where Ma Robison had the customary piece of apple pie set out for me. It's all wonderful, but the ten dollars have melted. . . .

I was sitting in the Kappa Alpha Phi rooms racking my brains and heard someone say, "Come on, play something."

Didn't feel like it. I had just come from making another tour of all the restaurants in search of a job and had had no luck.

"Aw, come on. Try *Pretty Little Baby*. Hilas wants to get his drums out."

"Has Hilas got a set of drums?" Why, Hilas to me was just Mr. Steinmetz the tailor's little boy. It never occurred to me he was interested in music. But there he was dragging a set of drums in the door, setting them up by the piano. I sat down and started playing listlessly. There were more important things at the moment than playing piano so the tailor's little boy could practice on his drums.

But the years in Indianapolis had not been in vain. There was the steady beat of my left hand and the slight accent of the upbeat—Reggie's trick. Hilas hit his drums.

In a moment I felt their rhythm. Gone were the worries, gone the thoughts of a job. I had never played with drums before and had no conception of the surging lift they gave. They were like a machine, a perfect machine that automatically placed my fingers on keys that I had never hit before. I *felt* jazz; I was improvising like Reggie and it was coming *right*.

The president of our high-school fraternity, the Kappa Alpha Phis, came in and stood listening for a moment. Then he stopped us. "Let's throw a dance tonight. I'll give you guys five bucks apiece if we take in that much."

Five bucks! A fortune. We agreed hastily and he called the fraternity houses and spread the word.

That night when Hilas and I walked into the twenty-by-forty upstairs hall, over a hardware store, there were twenty couples waiting.

I could play *one* piece with perfect confidence. A one-step. I removed my heart from my mouth and sat down. Those were my hands on the keyboard. I took a deep breath and hit the keys. The building began to rock and roll. The dance was on!

We went wild. After five choruses Hilas gave me the high sign to shut down with an ear-splitting crash of the cymbals.

There was applause, thunderous applause, and now

thirty couples jammed the floor. College couples from the Student Building dance. We are stealing their crowd!

"Who is the kid on the piano?"

"Boy, he can really go!"

"He has a different sound . . ."

"Hot piano . . ."

"Not ragtime . . ."

They had to turn couples away—and at a buck a throw.

The pots and pans in the hardware store below clanked and rattled dangerously. Everything moved fast; people, handshakes, hellos. I "helloed" myself to death. Somebody yelled for water; people were sweating! I was a physical wreck, and by twelve o'clock I could hardly drag myself out of the hall to get to Roy Beard's joint for a sandwich.

I was "local boy makes good" and thankful to Reggie, to Hube, to Ed East and Hank, the musical influences that made it possible.

Four years before this, by good fortune, we had lived in earshot of Hube's fraternity house. True, there came from there, sometimes, banshee whoops and yells—some doubtless emitted by Wendell Willkie and Paul McNutt; they lived there then. But more often came the sound of a piano.

And I could lie in bed at night and listen to Hube. He had a right hand that was a miracle of the times. He could run octaves at lightning speed, but I believe his bass made even a deeper impression on me.

The piano had me and sometimes I would look out and see a college student standing in front of my house listening to my version of *Maori*, copied from Hube.

When students passed by, to impress them, I'd really flail the old golden oak and accompany myself with much banging of the left heel.

And so I banged my left heel now and the pans clattered and clanked and the doorman tore his hair and turned away couples; Hilas is a "king" and the dance is a roaring success.

And I made five bucks. I could go on to school.

Our high-school fraternity dance that year was to be an important affair. We heard of a hot Negro band down in Louisville and we signed them unheard. And then spent three feverish days draping the new City Hall with banners, printing ornate programs, and talking of the coming of Jordan's band.

Perhaps Kate Cameron sensed a grand shindig that night and, so as not to miss it, she accepted a bid from this hundred-pounder and had me walking on air.

The big night arrived and there was a hush of expectancy when Jordan's men climbed on the stand. We listened to the introductory crescendo from the little black piano player as he tried out the action of the piano. He grinned, showing big white teeth, and hit a few chords of *Fate,* that masterpiece of minors. I laughed aloud. Something surer than hell was going to happen and it surer than hell did!

Jordan's men break into *Russian Rag* as a grand march. But nobody marches! We do a wild shuffle. And then they change the rhythm to a one-step.

I'm a Congo medicine man! Kate and I whirl. I'm wilting to the floor! Hilas Steinmetz has fainted dead away.

The word is "breakdown." Brought on by music—

disjointed, unorganized music, full of screaming blue notes and a solid beat.

To confess that I behaved that way, that this new music had this effect on me, is properly apt to give the impression that I was, to put it charitably, unbalanced.

But in those days, and the days to follow, jazz maniacs were being born and I was one of them. There were leaping legions of them from New Orleans to Chicago and Bloomington was right in the middle. Alleged to be in the exact center of population at that time and a part of the population was going jazz crazy.

What you have just read may be confusing to you. The wild leaps of time and space, back and forth, the varied people and varied things that keep cropping up doubtless seem out of place. But that is the way it is. I write from a memory of the events that made the firmest impressions upon me, more or less in the order of their remembrance rather than the order of their happening. As you mature, the long exciting days and years of your youth pass before your eyes as in a montage; a montage of the events that were important in making the real you— the *now* you. The *now* me is a composer, a song-writer. Unimportant as it may be, this little book goes on to tell what I was to experience to become that very thing. It is my answer to the question. Another writer's will be different.

So I remember that September morning of 1919 that followed the big dance. I had to cut the grass for Ma and Pa Robison. Had to be careful not to run the lawn mower into Ma's nasturtium bed, and be sure to trim the grass neatly around the little circular basins that held her long-stemmed roses.

The blade of the mower purred in an even pattern of rhythm—monotonous, yes, but crisp and real. The events of the night before were real enough—didn't I run into the clothesline pole thinking about them—but they were difficult to recapture in all their obscenity as I glanced down the street a block or two and saw Aunt Sadie's house standing there in quiet honesty. Simple, unchanged and unmoved. That other world, the one I didn't quite belong in was going along just the same. Jordan's orchestra hadn't made a dent in it. Inside Aunt Sadie's house were two newborn cakes; one for the Ladies Exchange and one for the neighbors and relatives to sample if they chanced to drop in.

Why don't you go down and sample her cake, Hoagland? She'd appreciate it. She lives in a kitchen, clean and respectable. Doesn't care one iota about your shindig last night—only cares about your health. She loves you because you are one of the men of the family. Young yet, but she doesn't see you that way. She sees you as the future president of the Monon Railroad, the one her Uncle Billy has worked on for twenty years. Go see her but don't tell her about last night. She won't understand.

Grass grows green and deep and the harder you push the faster the mental processes work too. Energy is sapped and there I lay in the shade of a quilt that hangs on the line. Took Ma 94 days to make that quilt. Could have won a prize. Didn't even enter it. Took me three hours to make five dollars playing a dance. Aunt Sadie got fifty cents for her cake and her two hours' work. It made me think. There will be lots more dances and lots more dollars. Whistle while you work, too. "No, Aunt Sadie, I don't think I'll ever be president of anything. Mother named me after a railroad president, I know, but it is too late now, I'm afraid."

Mother's era in popular music was ragtime. Her life was lived in ragged time, on the ragged edge, but she was always there. Eighty pounds of solid rock which nothing could dismay.

My father would have been happy driving a cab in Bloomington, when I was knee high to a bass fiddle, if he could have had a team in front of him composed of a couple of champion racing trotters. He lost trade, as it was, being the Barney Oldfield of the horse-and-buggy era; it was all much too slow for him. It is hard for a fellow to come back from a war and resume the old pace. It was hard for the veterans of my generation to come back from the Argonne and slow down to the prewar tempo. You get into a higher gear and you never quite drop back.

My father could turn a handspring when he was forty-five and he was middleweight champion of his regiment in the Spanish war. He was eying the heavyweight belt when he was demobilized.

But he was a sentimentalist, a softhearted one. It tore his heart out when my baby sister died. He arrived late at night from a trip to an Alabama boom town, desperately hoping that "diphtheria wasn't dangerous," to find the child in her little white dress. My mother played hymns on the golden oak, for no service was permitted.

Magic and heartbreak, and heartsickness too, go with that piano. All there was of the Carmichael family was stored in that piano, an Armstrong upright bought on long-term payments. We didn't have much, we weren't always awfully close knit, but the golden oak, with mother playing and all of us listening, entranced, kept us together—gave us something always to come back to.

And the Book Nook piano; the piano Reggie Duval played, beating out things I heard down to my feet. My mother playing *Maple Leaf Rag,* her hands so tiny, but reaching the octaves, and in them all the strength and power of a man's.

Looking back, I wonder at the tolerance and understanding of our neighbors. Imagine living next door to someone who hammered on the piano at all hours. Hammered out barbaric music, frequently bad and groping music even of its kind.

Of course those neighbors live all over America, kindly patient neighbors who suffer unprotesting, while the little Hoaglands of the land search the piano keys for what they think is beauty. They deserve an accolade. They are true patrons of the arts.

The Beiderbeckes were patrons of the arts. When I was collecting beer bottles, which the college boys threw into Dunn Meadow, and wistfully watching the big boys play football, Leon B. ("Bix") Beiderbecke was born in Davenport, Iowa.

Bix must have been something of a surprise to his parents; his strange character so apart from those solid Teutonic virtues the numerous Beiderbeckes in Davenport possessed.

A child whose brow was seldom dampened by athletic perspiration: he had other, less useful, talents. When the river boats came down and flashed the plume of steam from their whistles, he could walk to his piano and pick, from the 88 keys, the very note and very pitch that lingered in the air.

His family were musicians, but his own strange precocity must have baffled them—all but his mother, in whose eyes he could do no wrong. Their tastes were solid, classical. His tastes were catholic, but the tom-tom from the jungle beat in his pulse.

He fooled with drums awhile when he was older—discarded them. "I got what I wanted," he told his cousin.

And then one day he brought home a horn—an old-fashioned silver cornet. And they were married.

The lines of this, his true love changed . . . she became sheathed in gold later . . . a fine cornet and he was faithful to her until death did them part.

He heard the black men who plied the river and he learned what his love and he could do. And he did more. He didn't say these things. Maybe he didn't think them. But he expressed them on his horn.

"With that," he told his cousin, "I can do what I want to do." And then he reached the top and heard things in his head he *couldn't* do. And I think that killed him.

The years have pants! Mine are long again and I have five dollars in them. Five dollars earned from the boys who made me play. The boys for whom I *wanted* to play: Bloomington boys. And Bix has a horn.

Ed East was one of these boys and *Hello, Hoosier Town* was his own song.

"How do you write songs, Ed?"

"I don't know," Ed told me. "I don't know."

And he was right. No one ever knows. If you knew how to compose you wouldn't be a composer. You'd just be playing a little game of harmonies. And if you'll pardon me I'm afraid that that's exactly what some of the so-called "old masters" did. Result—no melody. You don't write melodies. You find them. They lie there on the keys waiting for you to find them. They have been there for centuries and you are a composer or a writer if you know when you've found one. If you've found the beginning of a good one, and if your fingers do not stray, the melody should come out of hiding in ten minutes.

Composing is as likely to be playing with emotions as with harmonies, and the emotions you play with, well, they are hopes and fears and lots of things.

I remember looking over Elephant Mountain in Missoula, Montana, and imagining I saw the smoke from the Bloomington gas plant. And maybe that heartsick pretense is in a song I've written. The kids in Missoula in 1910 were fine kids. The Bitter Root River was clear, cool, and full of fish. But, it wasn't Bloomington. We had "gone out west," seeking the opportunity that my dad never quite found. We didn't stay in Missoula long, but too long for this sadeyed little creature who longed for home.

Again while very young we went to Bedford, Indiana, to live. The Bedford Eagles, where my dad took me to show me off at the piano, drank the same beer they drank in Bloomington. But, Ed East didn't live there. Hank didn't live there. You didn't write songs away from Bloomington. . . .

"How do you write songs, Mr. Berlin?"

"Go away, boy."

He didn't say that, but probably wanted to.

This was in Palm Beach several years after the Kappa Alpha Phi shindig.

The president of one of the larger public utility companies gave parties in Palm Beach that were really something. The vintage champagne flowed, at these, as though he had an artesian well of the stuff. The guest list frequently included Billie Burke, the late Flo Ziegfeld, Irving Berlin, and others of comparable importance. I had left college to join a small band and we were playing private parties down there during the winter season.

I impressed one of the younger Wanamakers with *Nola* and *Canadian Capers* and with the dulcet approbation of a beautiful Follies girl and a generous cargo of champagne aboard I *really* impressed *myself*.

This is Hoagland Carmichael. Up among 'em. Got fifty dollars for it. Important as the kid who used to get into the show free because his mother played the picture-show music. Some better than making a buck a week ushering in Bloomington's Grand Theatre "nigger heaven." Or hustlin's pool to pick up a quarter at Tom Huff's emporium.

The same guy that used to run a cement mixer in Indianapolis twelve hours a night. Did you ever run a cement mixer? They pour the sand in, the cement, the gravel, and you spin the drum over and the water goes in; that big drum is turning all the time and you dump it out into a Georgia buggy and away it's hauled and then you spin the drum back and here comes the sand and the gravel and the cement and you turn it back as the water goes in and there is a guy standing there with an empty buggy. . . .

Fill her up; let's roll. All night long in December, in Indiana; water freezing to your pants, feet getting numb, twelve hours of it. And a big clock, a big ugly clock, up there that you can see. Clock breaks down every night and won't move, but you can't stop. The whole line stops if you stop. And the hands on the clock won't move.

Hands move pretty good, though, beating out *Canadian Capers* with a Follies girl draped over your shoulder and Irving Berlin listening. There's a hollow-stemmed champagne glass sitting beside you. Fill her up, my man, let's roll, the whole damn line breaks down if the piano player stops—but the time goes faster.

And Irving played his new song. With a feathery and uncertain feel of the ivories, but with lots of charm. I stopped, looked, and listened wordlessly, but I made a sudden firm resolve.

"Hoagland," I said to myself, "by God, if anyone who plays that feebly can write that nobly—you can write a song."

What were we talking about? Oh, yes, Bedford. We lived near a dump. No songs there—no golden oak. Not even much apple pie. Perhaps my unerring and instinctive urge to return to Bloomington conveyed itself to my mother and father. Maybe I said it aloud and often. Whatever it was, the Bedford excursion was whitewashed; eventually I was attending Bloomington High School and had played my first dance.

After the dance we swarmed to the Book Nook. Cokes and coffee and tense high-pitched enjoyment. Batty and Bruce De Marcus were there. I had known them as tough little redheaded kids who fought each other over a Daisy air rifle, and now they were back in Bloomington and they were saxophone players.

"Play, Hoagy," and someone pushed me to the piano.

I played for Batty and he played for me. When we finished, Batty was calling me dirty names and running his big freckled hands through my hair. We fell into each other's arms. Never had I dreamed of such notes as came from that horn—fast arpeggios and all of them tongued! Batty played an entire chorus and he took it on one breath. His face grew red and he gasped for air as he hit the last high note. This was Batty of the big hands, the red hair; the impulsive, talkative boy who two years later was as much a part of the New York scene as Wilson Mizner or Paul Whiteman. He was the 400's choice over Rudy Weidoff and he carried his laurels with a boyish charm. If he was walking up Broadway, toward the El Mirador Café, with his naked saxophone under his arm, and was behooved to take a pee, only Batty would stop a cab and ride two blocks to the Astor Hotel to do so.

The crowd in the Book Nook heard the combination and we were sold. We received two bids to play dances that night.

Have you ever seen the big maples? The trunks are sometimes three feet in diameter and they shoot straight up, barren of branches, for some forty or fifty feet and then they spread out into a huge umbrella of limbs and foliage. Hundreds of these and an equal number of large

beech trees shade the Indiana campus. For many years
there were no walks—just natural paths winding among
the trees. Several of these led to a street that borders the
campus on the east, called Sorority Row, and here is
where the quartets and jazz bands serenaded at night.

A low stone wall borders the campus on the south.
This is the "spooning wall" and is usually dotted by
quiet indiscernible couples late at night who have
stopped there on the way home from the Book Nook or a
picture show. To the north of the campus, bounding
Dunn Meadows and the old athletic fields, runs the famous Jordan River. Famous because of its high-sounding
name and yet its waters—a foot deep in floodtime—
barely trickle during the dog days of August. But never
let it be said that this jaded stream produced nothing. It
did. Crustaceans. Crawdads I mean, by the thousands.
We kids were not barefoot boys with rod and reel, we
were barefoot boys with tin can for scooping them up.
Fishing for crawdads is an art. It's like catching a fly with
your hand and almost as difficult. Indiana Avenue is the
other boundary and thereon stands the Book Nook.

The Book Nook was a little house originally. It was
situated hard by the campus on Indiana Avenue and it
really was a book store. Gradually it had grown and been
added to until it seated a hundred or so coke-guzzling,
book-laden, high-spirited students. There new tunes were
heard and praised; lengthy discussions were started and
never quite finished. There the first steps of the toddle
were taken and fitted to our new rhythm. Dates were
made and hopes were born. Jordan's band continued
playing for the local dances and sometimes they could be

prevailed upon to stay over and play for a Sunday afternoon session in the Book Nook. *"Shake it and break it,
and hang it on the wall"*—that was the Sunday ritual.

Let me take you gently by the hand and lead you
into the Book Nook on a normal afternoon. That little
guy, over there, flogging the piano—that could be me.
The one with the long nose and the exerted purple face.
And the large freckled youth with the saxophone, the
one making those long blue notes, that's Batty De Marcus. The high-cheekboned unshaved youth perched yonder in a booth, that's Moenkhaus, composing a poem,
perhaps, for we hear his weird coyote-howl laugh even
above our efforts.

A few couples are seated in booths at the far side and
Pete Costas, the proprietor, is punctuating his English
with Greek epithets because Klondike Tucker, the Negro
chef, has balled up an order.

Wad Allen is curved into a seat across from Monk,
and the thing he toys with, stroking sensuously, is a piece
of lemon meringue pie. All Bent Eagles love to pat a
lemon meringue pie—though blueberry will serve in a
pinch.

Those round yellow objects arising as the twilight
creeps softly upon the scene? Why, those are grapefruit
rinds hurled at me because my music has grown too
sedate.

I dodge the grapefruit rinds and stop. Monk is going
to read his creation. There is a moment of quiet. Quiet
fraught with expectancy. Nerves too tight. Minds keyed
to vistas beyond the horizons of so-called rational
thought.

Monk reads:

> Blooters, thou knowest no Heaven
> Blooters, thou knowest only us
> Bugs, men, whores and fowls—
> They are the Children of Heaven.

There are wild yells. Wad Allen shrieks his appreciation. I hear in my ear a voice. The voice of a non-Bent Eagle. It is a plaintive voice, timid with query.

"What does it mean?"

I turn and smile pityingly. This poor guy doesn't know what those immortal lines convey.

"It means just what it says," I hear Wad Allen say. "Just *exactly* what it says."

That's normal.

It is also normal for the Book Nook to be nearly deserted and for Moenkhaus and Wad Allen and myself, and Harry Hostetter too, to be there. We talk of things we are puzzled about. We confess bewilderment and doubts and fears and we never laugh at each other. We wonder where we are going.

"I'm going to be a lawyer," I say firmly. "Jazz is okay, but—"

Harry interrupts. "Thanksgiving come but once a dozen," he says, looking at Monk. "But what we call jazz comes but once."

"It originated in the South," Wad says, "Buddy Bolden blew hot jazz for the Creole dances. They get most of the credit for it."

"Jazz" meant "play it faster." Buddy put a hat over the bell of his horn to get fuzzy effects and Freddie Kepet, another Creole, brought his band to the Columbia Theatre in New York about 1911 and showed 'em how to use a mute. They liked their music more in keeping with their climate though—slow and raspy.

"I hear they put Buddy in an asylum," I say and I hope with all my heart that they didn't take his horn away from him. "Law is the best."

"Buddy Bolden, the Original Creole Band, and the Original Dixieland Band were preceded by at least two people I've heard of," Harry says. "One was blind Tom Harney. He was a sort of prodigy on the piano, around Lexington and Louisville . . . That was back in the eighties and early nineties . . . he was feeble-minded too. He played his real hot licks as an introduction to his concert. He was great, but he wasn't original except when he played it wrong—but, oh, so right—as an attention rouser."

"So what?" Monk says lazily. "Hogwash isn't any too bright, and he plays them all wrong. As a matter of fact," he admits modestly, "I am perhaps the greatest piano player who ever fell off the Matterhorn."

I like jazz . . . kinda like law too . . . like people. . . .

"I'm wondering what Buddy Bolden had in his brain when he blew the introduction to what is now *Tiger Rag*," I say.

Monk yawns. "Who cares? I'm going to die any day now."

And he did die. Just a year before Bix, also, strangely, the same year Buddy Bolden, now an old man, finally went to the place where nobody's crazy.

They got Buddy, but they never got us. A lot of people listened to us and were dubious and we knew it. But they never *proved* we were nuts.

We like to walk along the streets and see people watering their lawns and we like to hear the rumble of the ice wagon and the querulous barking of a familiar dog. These sounds are right. We *know* they are right and perhaps they make us afraid.

Certainly, we were a little afraid one night several years later in New Castle, Indiana. Our college band was at its peak and we were very full of our music and of ourselves. It got around to Christmas—the third Christmas for my last college band. The real band—"Carmichaels' Syringe Orchestra," we called it.

"Alas," Wad Allen says, "a herd of elephants are singing Christmas carols below our window."

None of us laughed, but we listened.

We have just played a dance. It is two o'clock in the morning and Wad has just come in. Somebody pulls the sliding doors in the dingy hotel room exposing an even dingier room, drab and cold.

There on a little table is a Christmas tree, dilapidated and maimed. One forlorn candle burning at the top of its scraggly branches. We stand looking at this little scrub and I finally muster all my courage to speak in an exaggeratedly deep voice.

"Well, well, look what we have here! Something for little Waddie Allen—cause he's been a good little boy. And here's a surprise for Artie Baker. . . ."

A potato grater for Wad. A piece of rope for Art Baker. Someone gets a funnel. It is too much for us. No one yells an inanity. No one speaks. We look at the tree and the single candle shimmers and flickers and is reflected in the tears that stand, suddenly, in our eyes. We stand there, six little children of jazz, brave in long pants, and then the candle sputters out and we are afraid.

After a moment someone says something and we laugh. A little laugh.

Hoagland, these guys are your friends . . . they are the guys you want to play for. They are the ones who make you play. There's Wad, and Bridge Abrams, and the others, who played the dance along with you, and even though you aren't going to follow the beat of hot sweet sound, even though you're going to be a lawyer with solid fees and solid arguments, they're with you, in this room, on Christmas night and somehow you aren't lonely. But they come back to you Christmases; always they come back, and other times too, they are with you.

The band, the college band—one for all and all for one—and it wasn't corny.

Moonlight nights you hear the ghostly laughter, the silver-gleaming sound, the good talk. Rainy nights you remember. Fall nights you recall.

I recall Bix, he of the silly little green horn and the golden flags of music that fly from its bell. He's making early jazz history playing with the Wolverines. The Wolverines are making a little niche in jazz legend never to be lost as long as records go around. The same old Bix who as a kid beat that piano when the house was all empty. Wouldn't play a note when the family asked him, but who'd go out on the river boats though and play the steam calliope if they'd let him . . . hang around the bandstand and pester hell out of the New Orleans honkytonk graduates teaching the nation jazz . . . if

they'd let him. Get home in the parlor among people that
loved him . . . wouldn't play a note.

And Monk, he of the pasty face and slow silly smile
in front of the weird swift mind. Founder of the Bent
Eagles. The surrealist of the campus. Wise and foolish,
sane and crazy, lovable and laughable. Perhaps too sane.

Hostetter, older than we are, a little. Been a lot of
places, seen a lot of things. Always in quest of that com-
fortable sandy isle—that golden fleece—and although he
never quite grasped them, you could lean on Harry's approbation like a solid thing, a wall of sustaining belief.
And Harry is always right. Never lived a righter guy than
Harry.

Wad Allen, a member of my band, a member of the
Bent Eagles; handsome, friendly, impulsive. Not as sane
as Monk, not as handsome as Robert Taylor, not as good
a musician as Bix, but good in his own way; a real personality behind a horn.

> If castor oil removes a boil
> And Oscar rows a goat
> Don't use your feet on shredded wheat
> Inhale it through a boat.

Monk and I were sitting in the beat-up Chevrolet
and he handed me the poem. He was then writing under
the nom de plume of Wolfgang Beethoven Bunkhaus.
It's 1923.

"I inhaled it all right," I said.

"What?" Monk asked.

"The Chicago style of jazz," I said. "George Johnson—he's from Chicago. I met him last year and I didn't know what the hell he was talking about till he showed me how he'd like to play a sax."

"You got a burn out of him?"

"Yeah, I met him again this summer. We got to talking and I got hold of a saxophone for him. He doodles like Batty, but he has a jerk in there every once in a while on the upbeats. He says only a few are doing it— the New Orleans Rhythm King at the Friars Inn in Chicago. It makes me weak, thinking about a whole band playing that rhythm."

"A lot of things make you weak," Monk said comfortably.

Monk had come back from Europe. We were just getting acquainted, anticipating, I suppose, the strength of the friendship that was to grow between us.

"Tell me more about him," Monk urged. "I can get it when you tell it."

"He ducks his head down to one side when he doodles, and when he plays. He only stresses the first and third beats of the measure, but, Monk, he rides you along."

"Why didn't you go on up and hear them play?"

"Took a job . . . Lake Manitou. The Syncopating Five had made a name for the spot; I was glad to get the offer."

Monk swung his legs out of the car and leaned back in the seat. "Good, are they?"

"Yeah, although they're not so jazz crazy as some of us."

"Did you do any good?"

"Do you remember big Ebe Grubb? The time he

played in Bloomington and listened to us and threw a chair out the window simply because he liked a couple of chords I used?"

Monk nodded.

"He met me at the station. He's got hands that can almost cover the banjo he plays."

"How'd you do? Did the customers go for it?"

"We hit all right. I told Ebe about George Johnson, and taught him the piece that George showed me . . . they call it sock time."

"I'd like to have heard you."

"Ebe went at his banjo like a gorilla. A lick set him swearing."

"Show me how you sock it." Monk was interested.

"Dood-dood-doodle, La-de-a-de-addle-la-da, sock that beat with your fist in your palm. Accent the down beat."

Monk doodled along with me; his fist hit his palm with the same sort of joyous accent that I loved.

"Makes you feel good," he said.

"It cured a guy up there in the band—a guy named Taz Walters. He sang for us and wore leg braces. Every day it was—'Taz fell! Pick him up!' In a couple of months he learned to play golf and threw away the braces."

Monk nodded his belief.

Hoagland, you seem to be like Huckleberry Finn, wanting to be Oliver Wendell Holmes and sit on the Supreme Court . . . or a big corporation attorney, with a battery of helpers and a yacht anchored in the East River. . . . Like Peck's Bad Boy wanting to play hot

music like Louis Armstrong. Or, writing the blues like
Handy or Clarence Williams . . . part dead-end kid
. . . part lawyer . . . part musician . . . Hoag-
land, what the hell's the matter with you?

Thoughts of this sort went through my head in the
fall of 1922 after I had met George, and I decided for one
final time to study for the bar. But I was restless.

I was in a hole for a band that fall anyway. The boys
I had lined up ran out on me to join the campus com-
petitor who could read music. *Hoagland! This law angle
is solid . . . you're cut out for it!*

The tedium of the fall was broken, by a wild ride on
a train, when we went to Boston to see the Indiana-
Harvard game. With ten dollars, borrowed from one of
the more warm-blooded professors, I buried myself under
the stacks of luggage and stayed there until we reached
Cleveland the next morning. The porter spotted me and
I had to win his confidence by buying his breakfast, after
which I managed to conceal myself from the conductor
by standing behind the toilet door and spending some
time in a locked linen closet.

Our spirits were high, and for a gag the team put
me in every music store window in Boston, where I
played the piano and was billed as the "shipwrecked dog-
faced boy wonder."

Indiana lost the game in a driving rain, and we went
home with long faces.

Restlessness was spreading like a disease and it was
at its worst among musicians. Some drank heavily,
changed bands frequently. Always looking, never finding, the perfect thing. When they weren't actually play-

ing they were bored. Their resources, aside from their music, were limited.

Look at their women, I told myself, when their beats and half-beats interjected themselves between me and the briefs I had spread before me. Traipsing around all over the country, one-night stands, same old shop talk, same old speakeasies. Meeting in dance halls, falling in love with the music . . . the music, not the guys . . . the horns they blow . . . not the talk they say. . . . *Hoagland, take a girl who'll settle down and make a home, and have a couple of kids, and sew with her fingers instead of beating out the half notes. . . . A girl like Dorothy.*
. . .

Not Dorothy Kelly, not that first love, back there in high-school days. Not so much the recollection of Dorothy but the recollection of the feeling Dorothy had called up within me. I had met her two years before this period of restlessness of which I speak.

It was when I re-entered Bloomington High way back in '19—and I felt old. Older than the little girls with pigtails and shy provocative smiles. Hilas sat beside me in study hall.

"Psst! Who's that bunch of sweetness across the table?"

"Dorothy Kelly."

"How old is she?"

"Fifteen."

"Jeez! Cute as the devil."

"She asked who you were."

"Really, does she 'go' for me?"

"She just wondered. Send her a note and see."

In a moment I shot a note across the table: "Hello,

Hilas says you're some kid—and I bet you are. Meet me in the hall, baby."

She read the note with studied indifference. I liked the way she turned her chin up. I decided to give her a play.

Hilas slipped a note to me.

"Hilas said you were nice, but I bet you're not. I won't meet you in the hall."

I waited for her on the stairs after school. I almost remember the pattern of the gingham plaid she wore. I do remember slim graceful legs sheathed in white cotton stockings. I remember that the stockings didn't wrinkle.

"You know who I am, don't you?"

"Oh, yes, Mr. Fresh-guy."

"Yeah! Well, I wouldn't mind having a date with you."

"Well, I *would*."

"I'd like to get acquainted."

"Mother doesn't allow me to have dates with anyone but Tony."

"But . . . Tony's just a *kid*."

"Yes. That's the reason."

It was nearly a week before she would let me come to her house to see her. A week of watching her in classes, keeping her in sight in the crowded halls—hearing about Tony taking her out in a car. Then, one day, she let me come to her house.

"I heard you play, last night. I was at the dance."

"Tony took you, didn't he?"

"Um . . . I love the way you play. . . . You and Hilas."

"Thanks. . . . I don't know much about music."

"Play . . . play for me."

"What?"

In the pattern of remembering, there was a song, the first tune, I suppose, that I was conscious of composing. I almost never remember it, but I can still play it. There weren't any words, and it runs along lightly, merrily, a thread of feeling holding it together.

Dorothy sat beside me and her cheeks turned a little pink.

"Why, that's lovely. . . . Did you really make it up for me?"

Afterwards we sat on the davenport and held hands. She let me kiss her once. I ran out of the house, not knowing why, but I was back in a few minutes, talking quietly with her through a bedroom screen. And then, I walked away and looked at her little frame house as if I'd built it with my own hands.

I was in love. Swiftly, surely, eternally.

But now two years have passed and I am restless. Maybe those strange notes from George's saxophone made me restless. Needed a change. To Chicago to hear the Rhythm Kings.

At the Friars Inn I found George and Vic Moore at a table. I was in a panic of anticipation by the time I had checked my hat. The clarinet player was wiggling in his seat. He started in on *Sensation Rag!* It was the doodle-style George had taught me. Then the cornet player picked it up and blasted his notes jerkily, with penetrating brassy tones. The notes smacked me at unexpected times and in unexpected places. They went right down through my gizzard and made my feet jump. George bounced in his seat like a trained seal.

Vic Moore laughed like an idiot and drummed the tabletop with his hands. He was a demented monkey, and George would try to calm him down.

"They're playing *Farewell Blues,*" George would say, "Oh, boy!"

"That's *Panama,*" Vic would say. "They're jig tunes from New Orleans."

"There's a kid out at Northwestern comes down and sits with them every night. Kid named Murray—Don Murray. We all sit in once in a while."

"They're the dopiest-looking bunch I ever saw," I said.

"They hit the weed. Some of them."

"Weed?"

"Yeah, marijuana . . . 'muggles,' they call it down in New Orleans."

"What does it do to you?"

"Things."

"Is it habit-forming?"

"No. Only a little . . ."

"Hell," I said, "Let's get some . . ." But I was interrupted by the arrival of a slight, extremely young kid who had just come in.

"Hoagy, meet Bix Beiderbecke."

"Hello," Bix said through slightly reddened lips. He didn't pay much attention, though his eyes and silly little mouth fascinated me.

When he had gone, George leaned over to me. "You ought to hear that kid play; he's going to be tops some day. He's got ideas, but his lip is still weak."

"Where's he from?"

"Davenport, Iowa. He's up here now going to Lake

Forrest Academy. He says he's liable to get kicked out any day, but not because he comes to town every night to listen to jazz bands."

"He's nuts about Ravel and Debussy's stuff."

"Sounds like a goof."

"He is. He used to go on the boats and play the steam calliope. Then he heard a couple of guys named Louis Armstrong and King Oliver." George stopped. "His folks wanted him to be a concert pianist. And has that kid got an ear! He can tell you the pitch of a belch!"

Soon the talk turned to Palm Beach. "Vic's family live down there," George said. He went on, expounding the virtues of Palm Beach, and in a few minutes it seemed to be perfectly reasonable to be planning a trip there.

"We'll play private parties, it'll be wonderful."

"Swimming in the ocean in wintertime . . ."

"Maybe we can get Bix to join us . . ."

I had serious doubts as to Vic's ability as a band manager, but a chance to play Chicago jazz with these boys overrode the objections put forward by my practical side. I agreed to meet them on the train in Indianapolis in two weeks.

Quitting school, Hoagland? Off to Florida to play Chicago jazz? What about Law School? The persistent prodding of my inner qualms made me uncomfortable. It made me think about thinking and realize that I did very little of that.

Remember the kid who rode so bravely back to Bloomington from Indianapolis with the high-school basketball team? That was Hoagland Carmichael wanting to be somebody. Wanting to be steady and solid. It isn't

*hard to be like other people, Hoagland, it comes easy
to you.*

It'll help with expenses. . . . I can go back to school
later, and I'll have money in the sock. Sock! Sock time.
George and I socking it together!

*But you've got a band at school. You going to run
out on 'em? You'd shoot anyone who did that to you. You
can't be a lawyer playing jazz in Florida. What in hell is
the matter with you? Lazy bones sitting in the sun.*

The atmosphere changed as we slept through
Georgia and when we pulled out of Jacksonville, for the
last lap down the coast, we were out on the back platform
singing *Chicago* and *Panama* to the station agents.
George and I had never breathed that ocean air before
and we felt great.

"Beats the cold damp air in Indiana."

"Sure do, man."

"Take those flag sticks and beat it out on the rail-
ing."

"Do-doodle . . ."

Our first impression of Palm Beach, acquired at
night, was slightly disappointing. But the next morning
was different. We threw on our clothes, like kids chased
out of a swimming hole, and rushed outdoors.

It was wonderful.

We kept right on running, trying to see everything
at once. We saw people riding around in wheel chairs and
we thought they were sick! We rented bicycles to run
faster and see more. It was wonderful.

It was so wonderful we didn't even try to get jobs for

ten days and then only because we were broke. But a job turned up.

There was a bar with everything from beer to absinthe; the tanned figures of the girls and the luxurious house inspired us. We had six or eight tunes down pat, and we had rehearsed a little. Our hostess liked our music and wrote us all checks for twenty dollars. But, our music didn't get over too well. The Dodges and Stotesburys were used to club music and our style was a little "advanced."

I got a burn out of it though, but soon the season wore to a close and Bix had never arrived. I was sad about that. They told me he was so great. However, I consoled myself, we knew a thing or two about jazz the crackers couldn't understand and even though a local long-underwear gang seemed more prosperous than we were, and worked more, we felt only pity for them.

Maybe it was for the best that Bix didn't come down, for if he had I would have stayed with that band—I know that. I would never have finished school and it was better as it worked out later.

I remember leaving Monk, folded up in a Book Nook booth and serious for once. "Hogwash," he said, "there are other things in the world besides hot music. I forget what they are, at the moment, but they are around." It was Monk's way of warning me. I remembered that. And I wanted to get back to Bloomington. Always back to Bloomington.

Vic and George wanted to get back to Chicago and get a band organized; they were going to call it the Wolverines.

We made getaway money in a small town in Florida,

booking ourselves as "The Country's Foremost Chicago Jazz Band"—a lie—and soon I was home again.

I remember trying to explain Bix to Monk. I remember trying to put Bix together for Monk, so that he would see him and hear him and feel him the way I did. It was like the telling of a vivid dream and knowing that it wasn't making sense.

"A man put the mark on him, Monk, marked him for greatness."

"A man with a horn. . . . What is man but a puny thing. . . . Best forgotten, all but the I. . . . The I as in Beiderbecke." Monk said.

"He was a black man with a golden horn and he played the boats, those floating palaces, that plied the rivers in the warm moon drenched nights of summer. The man was King Oliver . . . he played a trumpet."

"Not in this world?" Monk said, but he was listening.

"The boats came and tied up and the townspeople would go aboard and the boat would go down the river, ten miles or so, and then come back while the people danced or just sat on the upper deck and stayed cool."

"And little boy Bix, he blew his horn!"

"Yeah, he went on one of those boats one night and King Oliver was playing. After that he never was quite the same. He knew from that night on that the horn was for him, and he could say what he had to say on it."

"As a matter of fact," Monk said, "I am perhaps the greatest cornet player that ever drove a llama."

"I think you're the biggest liar I ever heard."

That same night I went to see Dorothy Kelly. Still beautiful . . . and we went for a long walk.

There is a beech tree on the campus of the University of Indiana, an old beech tree, cloistered by lesser of its brethren, mottled and scarred by countless intertwined initials.

Initials of those who would have the wish they make while carving them come true. For that is the magical property of this tree. Truly you wish while carving your initials and truly that wish will be fulfilled.

And it was there, that night with Dorothy Kelly, I paused. She was there beside and the wish was easy. To have her beside me always. Dorothy handed me her nail file.

The H was easy, two lines down and one across.

"What made you stop?" she asked.

Above where I was carving were two other initials, old and rounded with age. They were D.W. A local druggist's name popped into my mind.

Maybe he had put them there. He was a good man, a solid man. He was in his store early in the morning. He was in his store late at night. And doubtless in the chilly stillness of dark silent hours he had been there, filling a prescription for a doctor battling some illness that wouldn't wait for the conventional hour of opening.

D.W. led a life of solidity, of service. A good man.

But on the morrow I was to go away from Bloomington, into an exciting world, of no service and solidity, and so when the file had completed the H, I paused.

"I don't know," I said, suddenly miserable, and I put my arms around her, hard, "darling, I don't know."

I felt the beat of her heart and an errant gleam of light caught itself in her hair. But you can't cut yesterday on tomorrow. You can't cut your heart on a beech tree.

"I don't know, darling," I said again. "I don't know."

Christmas Eve in New Castle, with the little maimed tree, was somewhat different from the night I went up to Chicago to see Bix. It's the summer of 1923. We took two quarts of bathtub gin, a package of muggles, and headed for the black-and-tan joint where King Oliver's band was playing.

The King featured two trumpets, piano, a bass fiddle and a clarinet. As I sat down to light my first muggle, Bix gave the sign to a big black fellow, playing second trumpet for Oliver, and he slashed into *Bugle Call Rag*.

I dropped my cigarette and gulped my drink. Bix was on his feet, his eyes popping. For taking the first chorus was that second trumpet, Louis Armstrong. Louis was taking it fast. Bob Gillette slid off his chair and under the table. He was excitable that way.

"Why," I moaned, "why isn't everybody in the world here to hear that?" I meant it. Something as unutterably stirring as that deserved to be heard by the world.

Then the muggles took effect and my body got light. Every note Louis hit was perfection. I ran to the piano and took the place of Louis's wife. They swung into *Royal Garden Blues*. I had never heard the tune before, but somehow I knew every note. I couldn't miss. I was floating in a strange deep-blue whirlpool of jazz.

It wasn't marijuana. The muggles and the gin were, in a way, stage props. It was the music. The music took me and had me and it made me right.

Louis Armstrong was Bix Beiderbecke's idol, and

when we went out the next night to crash an S.A.E. dance where Bix was playing with the Wolverines, I learned that Bix was no imitation of Armstrong. The Wolverines sounded better to me than the New Orleans Rhythm Kings. Theirs was a stronger rhythm and the licks that Jimmy Hartwell, George Johnson and Bix played were precise and beautiful.

Bix's breaks were not as wild as Armstrong's, but they were hot and he selected each note with musical care. He showed me that jazz could be musical and beautiful as well as hot. He showed me that tempo doesn't mean fast. His music affected me in a different way. Can't tell you how—like licorice, you have to eat some.

Those incongruous times. Not long before the Wolverines could race our heartbeats, a member of the Utah state legislature introduced a bill providing a fine and imprisonment for those who wore, on the streets, "skirts higher than three inches above the ankle."

While we were doodling and weaving our own mystic pattern across crowded dance floors, audiences sat spellbound and quiet beneath the shadows on a screen. Marguerite Clark could bring a lump to your throat with the magic of her make-believe. The youngsters were calling them the "shifties." Elsie Ferguson and the Talmadge girls lived excitingly and bravely in the world of the cinema.

There was a "Red" under every bed, in those days, and the membership in the Ku-Klux Klan was rising by the hundreds of thousands. Rising highest in Indiana. Home of the brave and the land of the free. Right in the middle—remember that flagpole in Bloomington?

All over the country people were wildly playing

mah-jong. And a good many of us were listening, with all our hearts, to the steady pulsation of jazz. And then, the sudden change. People became restless. The music took on a down beat and illicit liquor flowed. Dances were "rat-races," women were "monkeys," and Dad was called "governor."

The years have pants. Ants in the pants. I wanted to go again . . . not for good, maybe, but right then. So I went up to Detroit and Jean Goldkette gave me a once-over and said perhaps I was a "comer." Being a comer didn't butter any bread, didn't even get bread to butter, and so, when Tommy Bassett, a violin player we'd met down in Florida, wired me, I left for New York for the rest of the summer at a lake resort.

George Johnson followed me a week later and we started selling the Ithaca folks our music. It was tough. They didn't take it. The hardest to please were the wine merchants.

They, on the other hand, had no trouble whatsoever selling their product to us. I remember one *inspection* trip we made with an old fellow through his cellars. I remember part of it . . . going in and sampling every kind . . . finding each one better than the one before it. But I don't remember going out.

His product also helped me get back to school.

When I left at the end of summer, determined to re-enter school in Bloomington, I was confronted with the problem of a desire for more bankroll.

Hoagy, pal . . . you can do this for Hoagland. You can make it up to him now. It's just a simple little prob-lem in arithmetic. You tote home a suitcaseful of real champagne, Hoagy, and, brother, you can make yourself a hundred bucks. You know all the angles, Hoag, old boy You're a cinch.

When I left I staggered under a cargo of the bubbling stuff.

Some people are destined to do great things, some are not. At any rate, my natural forte was definitely not along the lines of rumrunner. The trip home was one long sweat-drenched nightmare.

Every eye was an X-ray in the Hudson tube. Refusing all offers of help, I struggled with the damning suitcase alone.

Once on the Pennsylvania train that would take me to Bloomington, I got the bag situated and settled nervously in my seat. By the time I got to Pittsburgh I had to have a "coke" . . . must have a "coke" . . . so I got off and had it. I had forgotten to tell the train crew that I would be a little delayed so they went off without me. With my champagne.

Stone walls do not a prison make . . . but no one could have told me that. I frantically wired Columbus to have my luggage transferred to the next train, which I was on in body, though my spirits rode with those spirits.

Hoagy, I told myself, as sleep refused to release me, take it honorably, when they come to take you off this train. They may go easy on you . . . you're young . . . first offense. . . . You're just a little guy. . . . How much of a sentence do you get? Finally, I slept.

The next morning I stuck a trembling hand under my berth. There they were, my bags, untampered with. I gave the porter who had put them there five dollars and he grinned at me.

"You couldn't be no worrieder lookin', boss," he said, "if them bags was full of champagne."

I grinned too, but feebly. "I surer than hell couldn't."

The wine brought me a hundred dollar profit, paid my Law School tuition and my first month's fraternity house dues. That's me . . . a satchelful of bottles and a book full of torts. And the school was tough. My grades had something wrong with them, and the condition would have been more serious if I had not had the tender ministrations of my roommate. Not until a couple of years later, in the front row under the bold tutorage of Paul V. McNutt, were my grades of a respectable sort.

Monk and the Bent Eagles were making serious inroads on my sanity, and my battles with Property and Contracts frequently saw me come off second best.

I was glad to be home, though. I liked the boost Monk and Wad would give my depleted morale after one of these sessions with an exam. It was good to have Harry Hostetter's assurance that I had some talent. It was good to sit in the Book Nook and get reacquainted with that piano.

Monk was busy. He needed another outlet for his energies. Out of that need developed the Fishline Taxi Company. Wad Allen was his partner and they had a short and colorful career.

The home office was the Book Nook. The cab was a dilapidated Model T of brass-radiator vintage. The driver was called Jesus for short because he was the toughest in town. Business was acquired by hiring small boys to parade in front of the Book Nook and make fun of people for walking. Business came, but was often discouraged when Monk, taking a call for a cab, would reply lazily:

"Okay. We'll come over and pick you up today or tomorrow."

Soon the courts dissolved the Fishline Taxi Company and we were again dependent on the "Open Job."

The Open Job was a 1915 Ford that I had bought early in the fall of my first year in the university. It had served many years as a delivery truck and had been stripped down until there was nothing left but the chassis, a high front seat, and a boxlike affair that had been nailed on behind. All the fenders were gone and so was the hood. The Open Job was one of the first so-called "collegecars" in the Middle West, but I never allowed her beautiful sides to be marred by any wisecracks and, as a result, she responded gratefully every time I flipped the crank.

Most mornings during the winter I'd have to brush six or eight inches of snow off the motor before I cranked her up, but she always started and we would sail down Indiana Avenue on our way to an eight-o'clock class.

On a particularly cold morning you'd have to jump to one side after cranking her because she'd be frozen in gear. Once when I tried that, I missed her as she went by. I stood and watched my beloved boat go down the driveway under a full head of steam and head toward the campus. In the nick of time someone saw that the Open Job was without a hand at the tiller and did a bronco-busting act to get at the wheel and save her from an untimely end.

Only car I ever saw that would run without gas or

water and with the head cracked from end to end. We loved her dearly.

We had a band.

From the time that Hilas Steinmetz and I played the dance over the hardware store, we had a band. The personnel varied from time to time, though in college it was always pretty much the same. Those were deep and lasting friendships. So, too, were the friendships I had with my fraternity brothers.

Back to 1920 . . . that's an easy time to go back to, for actually I've never gone very far away from then. Back to the Kappa Sigma house and the friendships I sought there.

1920 was a big year for Indiana: the freshman class was the largest in its history . . . funny how each freshman class is the largest in history. They may be larger now, those freshman classes, but ours was the first truly "collegiate."

There was Wilbur from Huntington. . . . Jack, the tough egg from Terre Haute; Keller, the South Bend Dutchman with a long bird-dog nose; Stu Gorrell from Bremen and Pink Cadou and Louie Mitchener. Louie, particularly, had shaped up quickly from the greenhorn we had first pictured him and when we dressed him up in a borrowed tuxedo we discovered that he was the handsomest man in the house.

These boys were popular with the upperclassmen, except when the grades came through, and they upheld the social prestige of the house on the campus. Music was not a dominating factor among this crowd and it made

for fast friendships. Musicians are sometimes good bud-
dies, but not real friends.

By the time we were juniors we had well established
another order. That of "Friends and Sitters." We all sat
a lot in front of the fireplace and slung the bull. "Go to
work" meant "grab a chair, boy, and toast your shins."
Poor Pink! Once he hit the chair after lunch he was a
cinch to miss his one-o'clock class.

Those years with pants, when the pants were football, track, or very short for basketball as the season drove
forward. Those borrowed pants—borrowed from Pink,
who had had the forethought to get a pair pressed but
had not had the forethought to hide them securely out of
sight and reach of a "brother."

And the noise. The noise that never quite leaves
your head if you have lived in a house along with thirty
odd and exuberant guys. And the smells . . . flat beer and
acrid ashy air drifting toward you, as you cling to a last
few moments' sleep after a "bull session" that kept you
all awake the night before. The odor of wet basketball
shoes and old catchers' mitts.

The smell of that particular hair lotion Louis doused
on his head and which came from the steaming bath-
room . . .

And the talk. The talk of classes and lasses, and pass
the molasses . . .

"Get your ass out of bed, Hogwash!"

You scramble from the covers and fight for a chance
at one of three washbasins. . . . Lousy breakfast, Spanish
class . . . more classes. A chance to stand too close to that
cute little dame on the steps . . . lunch on creamed chip
beef and potatoes.

Announcement: There'll be a meeting of the freshmen in the card room imediately after lunch.

"What have we done now?"

"Shoot me, I dunno."

"You guys have got to watch your table manners.
And tomorrow this house is gonna be cleaned *right.* It
looks like the inside of a tornado. . . . Unnastand?"

A dull science class . . . back to the house under strict
orders: "You have to study. It's got to be quiet around
here."

Five o'clock. White shirt for dinner . . . borrow a
guy's tie . . . string beans and round steak.

"What does that cook try for, anyway? Can't she just
cook meat instead of *tanning* it?"

"When you gonna pay me that six bits, fella? I gotta
heavy date and I'm going to need it."

"Ten-thirty! Get your ass in bed, Rhinie."

The wonderful weekends. Housework all done.
Football practice, the Theta front porch . . . the Book
Nook . . . the phone ringing and the resultant rush to
make a date.

The Tri-Delt hop. Benny Benson singing *Cuban
Moon.* Hurry and get your date home before twelve-
thirty. Back to the Book Nook. Somebody has a pint.
"Play the piano for us, Hoagy." Dwight Van Osdale
reaching to the big yellow moon for the top notes of
Love Me and the World Is Mine.

The years have pants. Sometimes you have to make
them do for four years and sometimes, like me, you de-
voutly hope that you keep on growing. Four years with
the friends I had wanted so desperately, and found so sat-
isfying. The bands and dances, and the crises, and the

music that kept coming out. And then the night Harry Hostetter ran nearly a mile to get closer to hear it because he had hunted it all over the world and then had found it in Bloomington.

PART TWO

The course of a wandering mind and an unreliable memory is erratic. The path of this piece is helplessly jagged from an absence of chronology.

However, there is a time. There is *one* time, a little fraction of an era, to which my mind reverts. I can remember that time clearly.

That is the spring of 1924.

I expect that Bix brings this about. He of the funny little mouth, the sad eyes that popped a little as if in surprise when those notes showered from his horn.

The spring of '24. Seems like the moon was always out that spring . . . seems like the air of those nights was doubly laden with sweet smells. The air was thick and soft and pale purple. Grass was greener . . . moon was yellower.

Of course it helps to be young, and I was young.

Take a drink of whisky that tastes like kerosene in your mouth and a blowtorch going down. "Best I ever tasted."

"Wonderful. Have another, Hoagy, and turn the record over."

The Wolverines had played a dance on the campus —one of ten dances I had booked for them—and Bix and I were lying in front of the phonograph early in the

65

morning. We were playing the "Firebird" music of Stravinsky.

"Wonderful. Have another slug."

"What's wonderful?"

"Music."

"Sure. Whisky too."

"Guy used to be a lawyer."

"Who?"

"Stravinsky."

"Naw, Rimsky-Korsakov touted him offa the law."

"Touted him offa the torts, huh?"

"I dunno who he slept with."

"I said torts."

"Hell, I've slept with tarts myself."

"It's wonderful. Wonderful. Let's have another
drink."

"Sure is. Turn the record over."

There was a long silence. "Why'nt you write music,
Hoagy?" Bix asked softly.

"Naw, you're the one that writes the music. Every
time you put that horn up to your mouth you write
music."

"You write music, Hoagy," Bix said again like he
hadn't heard me.

"You write yours different every time."

"What's wrong with that?" Bix asked. "I like it different. Like Rimsky-Korsakov. He heard this Stravinsky,
told him to give up the law . . ."

"The torts . . ."

"Leave that crummy joke alone," Bix said. "I got
that crummy joke."

"Stravinsky study law?"

"Sure. Young guy like you. He studied law then Rimsy—ah, hell, you know who I mean—he told him to write music. So he wrote his. They dance to it."

"Dance to it?"

"Sure." Bix got up and did an entrechat, fell down and lay where he fell. I turned the record over. "Ballet," he said. "Hell, it's wonderful."

"Sure is," I said. "Give me another drink."

We lay there and listened. The music filled us with some terrible longing. Something, coupled with liquor, that was wonderfully moving; but it made us very close and it made us lonely too. With a feeling of release and a feeling of elation . . . and a feeling of longing too.

Silence. The record had come to a stop. A long silence and I was afraid to speak; afraid I'd spoil something. I can see Bix now, lying there, the music still playing in his head and me knowing it . . . afraid to speak; afraid I might spoil a note.

Finally I spoke. A little shyly. "I'm learning to be a composer."

"Who's teaching you?" Bix asked idly, rolling his head on the floor so he could look at me.

"Everybody," I said. "Everybody's teaching me to be a composer. I learned to be a composer a long time ago. Every time I see a pretty girl I learn more how to be a composer. Every time I play a Bucktown dance I learn how to be a composer."

"Nothing wrong with you," Bix said, "except you're drunk."

"So're you."

"I never said I wasn't." He stopped. "Music kind of

hits together in your head. Hurts you across the top of your nose if you can't blow it out . . ."

"But you can't blow it all out."

"You can try."

"Bix," I said.

"Yeah."

"Like what . . . kind of like with a girl . . . ?"

There was another long pause. Bix started up the phonograph and we lay there and listened to the music. Bix wasn't thinking about what I had asked him.

He was feeling something, though, and I was, too. It was the same thing but we couldn't put the words to it. It disturbed us. Ours were a medley of moods.

"Kind of," he said, but he hadn't thought about it.

"Like going first to school when you are a little kid and being scared?"

He nodded, narrowing his eyes and looking at me.

"Like a quick storm comes up on the river . . . and a horn . . . Maybe Armstrong or Oliver, and the storm . . ." he said.

"Put on the next record, let's have a drink."

"Like playing a steam calliope on a river boat with it hot as hell and the people dancing, all wet with sweat. Like blowing a horn," Bix said. "Like blowing a cornet. Like blowing a cornet."

"Bix," I said, "I'm gonna play a cornet."

"Sure. Everybody ought to play a cornet. Fun. Let's have a little one."

We had a little one and the sound washed over us as we lay there . . . two kids, kind of drunk, full of something and not able to put the words on it. But together, awfully together.

"Funny little horn," I said. "I'm gonna play me a horn."

You ought to go down to a music store sometime and pick up a record. Bix and His Gang. . . . Bix and His New Orleans Seven. . . . Bix and His Harmony Boys. Pickup recording orchestras that never played together except in front of a microphone to make a record. Dream bands, really. Dream stuff they played, too. They'd go over in the morning and meet at a studio and make a couple of sides. Play all night, sit up until ten in the morning, get in a soundproof room and fool around and then the technician tells them to go and away they go. Away they go. Away.

Wake up, though, spring of '24. That fine year, the year of the yellowest moon, the greenest grass, and the hottest music. The year you heard all the horn there was and still there wasn't enough for you; there wasn't enough for Bix.

You can't blow it all out . . .

You can try.

Wake up in the Kappa Sig house.

You can taste Stravinsky in your mind. Firebird. Firewater. Taste the kerosene in your mouth.

And who is that guy across there, sleeping in his underwear?

Why, it's Bix. Nothing immortal about a pale blond guy needing a shave sleeping in his underwear with his funny mouth open.

"Bix."

"Yeah. Go away . . ."

"Get up."

"My mouth is stuck together. Get me some water. Go away."

"I thought you wanted some water."

"Go away, get me some water."

"Get up."

"I'm trying," Bix said. He gets up and looks around helplessly. "Clothes."

"Here."

"Too small, I'll wear my tux."

"Can't do that. I'll find some others," I tell him.

"Okay. Water."

"In there."

"Jesus. Where'd you get that whisky?"

"I dunno. Good, wasn't it?"

"Lemme have your razor."

"Wash your face."

"Jesus, I cut myself," Bix said, scraping. "Where are my shoes?"

"You dressing?" I ask him.

"I'm trying."

And then we are quiet. The mumble and fumble of a hangover, the uncertain hand, the quivering eyelid.

Slowly we walk downstairs and out into the sunlight and all at once it's fine. There sits the Open Job, quietly waiting, faithful.

"Get up there and yank the spark down and ease up the gas when she catches."

"Okay."

"Naw, I'll choke her down here. There she goes. Choke her while I get around. No! You killed her."

"You killed me with that whisky. Who made that whisky?" Bix asks idly, twiddling the spark lever.

I go back to the crank, knee it in, pull out the wire loop of the choke with my left hand and give her a quarter turn. The Open Job roars to life and I leap to her controls before she dies. We sail down the street.

The good spring air, soft and cool in motion, blows the fumes from our heads. It blows away the hangover and it blows away the night before, the music, the things we strove to put into words.

Just a couple of average boys tooling down Indiana Avenue in an old open Ford, our minds pleasantly unoccupied, well pleased to be alive, surveying with appreciation the familiar scenes of a small-town Sunday morning. The people coming from church, content and unafraid, dressed in their best, at peace with their world as we are with ours.

We wander up to the Book Nook and dismount. Monk lolls at the front. Watching the scene, his eyes different windows for a different brain. A man is driving by in his car. Monk looks at him and drawls, "Look at that guy riding around with his kidneys."

We look at the man in the car and suddenly for an instant we see him like Monk sees him. It is grotesque and we put the vision from our mind and wander into the Book Nook.

Monk sits down limply and starts talking to Harry Hostetter about Teapot Dome.

All is not hot music . . . unstudied madness. Monk and Harry are as indignant over the theft of oil from the government as the people walking home from church.

We never put oil in the Open Job, but we are interested in it, too.

Coolidge is president, business is sound, things are all right, with a few notable exceptions.

But gradually talk goes back to things we *really* care about.

"What are you going to do this summer?" Harry asks Bix.

"I think we got a job in Indianapolis."

"Whereabouts?" I ask.

"The Casino Gardens," Bix tells him.

I look at him and wonder. Last night I have a deep conviction that this vessel of immortal music is something very precious; something that I must protect.

This morning he is a badly shaved kid with a funny little mouth, not very much to say. The great Bix is just another guy. But then I hear those pealing notes in my mind and I know he's not just another guy. What is he?

With that horn up there to his mouth and turned loose for thirty-two bars he's a great composer, that's what he is. He puts his stamp on every note and that stamp has no duplicate.

"You going back to Indianapolis this summer, Hoagy?" Monk asks.

"Yeah. Write me care the Casino Gardens."

Bix looks at me and smiles a shy smile of appreciation.

"Play something on the piano, Bix," Harry asks.

And suddenly I am fearful, I had heard Bix fiddle on the piano and I am reluctant to hear him play. "He's a cornet player . . ." I begin.

"He can play the piano," Harry says, looking at me sidewise, "you know he can."

"Just a little," Bix said, and he went over and sat down.

It was a terrible thing to watch. He was playing something of Ravel's and he could play only parts of it. His fingers were stiff and they seemed to go the wrong way—like a cat stretching a slow paw to find a note that wasn't there. Chords I'd never heard, little odd-shaped chords that shouldn't be played on a piano. They were pretty even if they did make me squirmy.

And at that moment a terrible desire overcame me. I had expressed it the night before, but I had forgotten it. Now it was an obsession. I wanted to play a horn. Bix could play the piano, maybe I could play a horn. I wanted to play a horn badly.

I did. I played it badly, all right. I blew my lip to a shred, blew my fraternity brothers right out of the house. Hiding the cornet in a chandelier didn't stop me, but one thing did. I quote a clipping from the university *Daily Student:*

SCIENCE CURBS HOGWASH MCCORKLE'S CORNET

In two minutes the sucking of California lemons achieved the end that forty deafened men failed to accomplish in a period of several weeks. Hogwash's cornet is banished.

Hogwash was puffing his cornet, his eyes and cheeks were bulged and his massive body was writhing to the rhythms of the horrible musical blurbs emanating from the muzzle of the instrument.

At that point six scientifically-minded youths filed into the room silently and stood in solemn and sinister poses. Hogwash McCorkle raised his eyes and continued blowing. Then—at a signal—the six produced lemons and sucked them. Hogwash's jaws began to ache and his lips puckered. A faint wheeze was all that came from the horn.

After this a stock of lemons was kept on hand and I'd have to drive to the country in the Open Job to practice in the shade of a kind old tree. I carried the horn around with me like a baby and at night I put it to sleep in its cradle, an old faded green velvet case.

I remember that our own band played the Senior Siwash—the last dance of the year on the campus. I took the cornet along to that one to show the lads a thing or two. I showed them so well that I had considerable difficulty collecting the money for the engagement. The other members of the band were in tears, but I was not convinced. And to this day I think the cornet was my instrument.

But that is what Bix would do to you. You heard him and it threw your judgement out of kilter.

The Wolverines, booked in by me, played dances on the campus almost every weekend that spring. I was a band leader, had a good band of my own, but I worked harder getting engagements for the Wolverines than I did for my own.

"I'll say," Wad said. "What a booker! If he couldn't get two engagements for the same night we'd have to shoot it out with the Wolverines."

"You always got paid," I said indignantly.

"Sure," Wad said. "Eventually, and sometimes in Confederate money."

"That's a base libel."

"We shouldn't be called the 'Collegians.' We should be called the Coolies," Wad went on. "Coolie wages . . ."

"Hogwash wouldn't hold out on you," Monk said surprisingly. "He just doesn't understand there aren't two Saturdays in each weekend."

"I make an occasional mistake," I admitted. "But look who I've got to try and sell."

We loved our band. Got along together better than any bunch of guys I ever saw. In spite of being a bad booker—forgetting dates and what not—the boys sometimes would bow down to me in a mock gesture of obedience and respect before blasting out *That's a Plenty* or *Tiger Rag*. Sometimes we'd bow down to Billy Little's banjo and bring it offerings of bright-colored serpentine.

Only once did we quarrel. Chet had missed a train—no drummer. Billy was drunk and wouldn't put on the ever-lovin' tux. Boiling inside, I picked him up by the buttons on his overcoat, stood him in a corner and slapped his face with a wet towel. He dressed. But the seed grew and later Wad said to Baker, "Why don't you learn to play that goddam thing?"

"Why don't you ever play in tune?" parried Baker.

But it blew over and we went to Muncie to play for the fleahoppin' kids at a hotel. Hopping from side to side like kangaroos, these kids made the walls ebb and flow.

Pants! Pants! So you finally go to your rooms and take off the pants and rest. Rest? As we were about to close the door a blonde dame of questionable appearance passed our door and smiled. Immediately a chorus of voices rang out:

"Boy! Did you see that?"

"Hot dog!"

"She's in the next room!"

"Boy! I'd like to go over there!"

"Say, guy, watch me!"

"I saw her first!"

"Naw, you didn't!"

I had my doubts about everybody being so eager to go into the girl's room, but there was such a fever of excitement that I suggested we make up a pot of $2 and draw straws to see who'd get to go. Luckily, the one who had raved most was the winner, so I handed him a two-dollar bill, an oddity at that time, and away he went with appropriate gestures and remarks from the side lines. We waited breathlessly for his return. He was gone quite some time, but finally appeared with a grin on his face. Eager questions were fired at him from all sides and he answered with a few cocky words:

"Well, she was pretty good. I've had better."

It didn't sound too kosher to me and when I walked over to his dresser to turn out the light I took a peek. Sure enough, there was the edge of the unused two-dollar bill sticking out from under his address book and keys.

But right now Bix and I have a hangover and he has just played the piano. Monk missed his class on account of that, so he sat down and did some scribbling.

"We'll have a class of our own. Here, Hogwash, read the questions. It's the Wheatena Test," and as he read it he stared straight at Bix.

Bix twisted his mouth into a distortion of approval and I read:

1. Spell Wheatena in four different directions.
2. What horse when it rained.

3. Define freight luner, and amelia.
4. Tell all you know about vetter.
5. Tell all you know about the defeat of New Mexico.
6. Write a short diary about skates. Leave out page three.

This agonized us and finally Bix's voice came up softly, putting his own strange phrase of approbation on the test. "I am not a swan," he said.

The friendship founded there between Monk and Bix endured to the end. Bix, the inarticulate kid, who played the wonderful horn. Monk, the surrealistic intellectual, who looked at the world through a glass that threw it into a hopeless distortion. Bix, the lone wolf, shy, silent. Monk, the campus character, who had a phrase for anything. They were friends. They understood.

It was good that Bix understood, I was glad. Once again he didn't let me down. So I took from my pocket and read a play of Monk's that had appeared in a student paper—the *Vagabond*—and watching Bix I saw that same strange sheen of madness appear on him as it had appeared on me when I first read the play.

"I am not a swan." He tried to say with those strange words all the things he couldn't say, and for us he was successful.

So here we are together listening to the beat of our hearts, full of feeling for each other, expressed as in words purposely foreign to those feelings. . . .

We are all right, pretty good bunch of guys. And I am learning to be a composer.

Hell, I was a composer.

Ever since I had heard Berlin down in Palm Beach I

had been a composer. Only trouble was I hadn't composed anything. So I composed something.

I went into the Book Nook one day and I sat down at the piano. Then I got up and ran my fingers through my hair. Sat down again and played Zez Confrey's *Kitten on the Keys* that I had learned from a record. Then I doodled aimlessly for a while. Went over and drank a coke. A "god-awful coke." Got kind of excited and went back to the piano.

The Wolverines were coming down again next weekend to play a dance. I would compose a piece for them. Or would I? Here it is the beautiful spring of '24. Awful good year to write music. But it didn't write itself. I fiddled at the piano. I just *had* to write a tune.

I got a phrase and played it. Played it again. And again and again and again. Pete Costas was frantic. I was emptying the Book Nook. The students, after profane pleas that I play something else, were leaving in droves.

Finally the Greeks prevailed. They drove me to the street. I made my way to the Kappa Sig house and started driving my fraternity brothers crazy, Same thing, same thing, same thing. But before supper I had it! Well, I had something.

The Wolverines were in town and Bix came over. I played it for him.

"It's swell . . . got four breaks. Call it *Free Wheeling,* Hoagy." And a Bent Eagle look came to his face.

Four breaks, one for each of us.

Others of the Wolverines drifted in. "We'll record it for Gennett." They got out their instruments and made the arrangement on the spot.

"Here, go here . . ."

"Bix, take this note."

"Okay, Jimmy, fake it for sixteen."

"You take the break this time, George."

George Johnson got me out of bed a week later and played the record.

I listened to it, silently. But there was no thrill there; I could have cried. "It's a good arrangement," I told George.

"Hell," he said, "it's elegant. It's in there, boy."

"Did you ever go to a graduation, George? Maybe your little sister was getting out of high school?"

George nodded, nonplused.

"That's the way I feel," I told him. "Kind of proud, but kind of sad too. It doesn't give me the old burn. And it ought to."

"Why doesn't it?"

"Well, I never listened to my own music before. I guess I don't know how to react."

George looked downcast. "How do you like the title?"

"I liked it, but *Free Wheeling* would have been okay, too."

"But *Riverboat Shuffle* is a good title . . ."

"Maybe it is, but let's talk about something else."

"Write me care of the Casino Gardens."

I took it kind of easy in Indianapolis, and why not? I was a composer and royalties would be rolling in one of these days. Easy to become a composer. Hell, nothing to it. All you have to do is sit in the Book Nook and write something, show it to the Wolverines, wait till the record comes out and sit on the front porch and one day open a

letter from New York. Important-looking letter. Let's
see, who's it from? Irving Mills; never heard of the guy.

"Dear Hoagy: We have heard the Wolverines' record of *Riverboat Shuffle* and we wish to publish the piece.
Enclosed is contract with Mills Music," etc. etc. Hell,
nothing to it. Hoagland, the lawyer, didn't even notice
that there was no promise to publish, only a promise to
pay royalties IF they did publish. But I was happy.

Easy? Yes, when the tune is right. What was it
Reggie Duval said and Harry Hostetter never let me forget? Oh, yes, "never play anything that ain't *right*. You
may not make any money, but you'll never get hostile
with yourself." I thought about it and loved them for it.
And I dreamed about how I would spend some of the
royalties. By that time I had forgotten that it had taken
twelve years of solid piano pounding, the happy moments,
the hard ones, the help of a friend, and the patience of
the neighbors to produce that little tune. It was that easy.

The Casino Gardens were an open-air paradise on
the outskirts of Indianapolis. The floor was surrounded
by gay umbrellas and the moon was close for the floor
was open, situated on the highest bank of the white river.
The orchestra played from a tiered platform under dim
lights.

I can still see this lovely scene. The smartly dressed
boys and the white-clad girls, their big hats making ever-
changing patterns as they moved to the music under the
big yellow moon. These people danced because they
loved to dance, gliding silently so as not to miss a wicked
note or beat of that band up there.

The Wolverines.

I would sit across from the band and their music would come to me slightly muffled. They were at their best playing lowdown and dirty but sometimes Bix would cock his head to one side and pop his eyes and then would come a shower of notes of such beauty they would send the dancers back to their tables as though they were sleepwalking.

Oh, those banners of melody cutting through the soft summer air. I can hear them still.

Bix would hunt me up during intermission and by way of taking a breather we would find a secluded corner where we could doodle *Riverboat Shuffle* or *Copenhagen* without interference. I'd doodle the melody and Bix would pump the bass and imitate cymbal licks.

Doodling was a favorite pastime of ours. And what is "doodling"? Why, it's what the Four Mills Brothers introduced years later and made a fortune doing. *We* didn't think it was commercial. In fact we didn't think. It interferred with our doodling.

The disintegration of that great band began that late summer. Vic Moore, he of the walrus mustache, vacated the drums in favor of Vic Burton, who booked the band into Gary, Indiana, and later the Roseland ballroom in New York, where they failed to draw crowds. Their failure in New York is considered one of the great mysteries in all jazz history.

The next I heard of Bix he had jumped the band to join an outfit in Chicago. Jimmy McPartland, who took his place in the Wolverines, blew a great horn but the band was slated for extinction.

A few days before the fall term opened at the university, in the fall of '24, I received letters from members of my own little band informing me they were all waiting to take up where we had left off the year before. Billy Little's letter was one long tale of bitter hardship. He said he was now a family man and possessed only a bad cold and comparable tuxedo. Chet Decker, the drummer, informed me he had made his place in the ensemble secure by painting my name on his drums.

Monk and Wad had gone to Michigan to play at a lake and had carried the flaming torch of Bent Eagle with them into the cold and pagan north. Wad Allen wrote as follows:

My dear Mr. Bolt:—

We have a new mascot for our orchestra. We keep it in the back end of an automobile. You can't guess what it is and neither can we, but we call it Moby Dick. It was found last Saturday morning on our way to play for a breakfast dance. If George hadn't thrown his bass horn at me we never would have found it. He bent his horn all to hell, but we found Moby and we are going to buy him a case. We have already got him a hat and some pretty ribbons. At first we did not know it was Moby. We foolishly thought it a bass horn rack, but when we were conducting the Whale hunting number at the breakfast dance and we were all down on the floor singing and looking for stray whales, we recognized him. I mean Moby. You really should see Moby; we have him all dressed up now, but the Serenaders (an alleged band working up here) are jealous of him and they try to steal him from us. But we take him on every job and when we are not working we hide him in the car. But, please, don't tell anybody this because the Serenaders are *very* jealous and would kidnap him and kill him or hold him for ransom.

Some people think he is an old Christmas tree which has been partially burned and which has only a few charred limbs remaining, but *we* know better—it is Moby Dick.

The Serenaders are spreading the word that we are all stool pigeons. We do not have to tell people what they are for everybody knows—it is a bad, bad, word.

I am writing to you on account of Mother's Day. Did you get your candy? You are the most wonderful woman in the world.

I sure enjoyed your letter. We all did. We have engaged an Hawaiian to make a group of animal solos. McHugh's music is able to be up and about now. He's been having pimples in his music, you know. Monk is still with us. I know that man and know that he is a damn fine man. We have a tune called *For Christ's Sake Potatoes.* It is a beautiful thing. We also play one named *Pullman Hotel,* another one called *Dictionary* and for an encore one titled *After I Say I'm a Wheel.* The numbers are all magnificent and we have the best band in the world. I am the booker. They are all good, but I am the best. Why don't you write me a letter?

Adamantly,
Col. Henry B. Wathall

I put the letter down and felt my throat tighten. Had Wad kept the little charred Christmas tree we had in New Castle? Had he kept it in the back of his car all this time? Why, by God, he had!

So I went back to school lighthearted. Nice to be back. And I was in glory with a new Ford equipped with all the gadgets and sporting real balloon tires. And as I had hoped the gang were all there and prepared to go.

We had, the year before, provided music at the Indiana Theatre for the comedies and newsreels and the manager of the theater renewed our contract. It was a lot of fun. The students would gather in the front row and if they thought our music wasn't good they would shower us with peanut shells and what other objects came to hand.

When the debris fell too thick and fast we'd switch to our sure-fire arrangement of *Alabammy Bound*. That would usually abate the storm.

In six weeks mid-term exams were upon us and my grades were of a middlin' sort.

It made me a little blue. Kind of blue and the blues hummed themselves through my mind; dismal little snatches in slow tempo. Kind of blue . . .

I stopped in the Book Nook one morning after class and the mood was on me thickly. Blue mood. Mac Mc-Carthy, having his regular morning spasm on the piano, only made me sadder, though Mac's technique was the most ludicrous I'd ever seen. When he got hot he flapped his hands like a chicken's wings and drooled slightly from the mouth.

On this particular morning he was going good. I stood and watched somberly as he gradually wore himself out.

"Take it, Hoagy."

I sat down, extended my arms in an imitation of Mac and started playing a hodgepodge of my frustrated feelings.

I struck a peculiar strain.

Mac caught it immediately. "Do that again, boy," he said, and he beat out a slow hesitant rhythm on top of the piano.

I was working like mad now. I changed the rhythm

to a fox-trot; then back to waltz time. Then back again. I was excited and in the crowded Book Nook I was alone. Classtime came and departed. Lunchtime came and departed. I sat at the piano.

When I finally finished the main theme I discovered it had only seventeen measures.

"Only seventeen measures," I said.

"I never heard of that," Mac said.

I worked then on an interlude, an odd chanting theme that had occurred to me. Mac stood beside me, his rhythm beats on top of the piano spurring me on.

"I got that."

"Sounds good," Mac said, excitement in his voice, too. "But what about an introduction?"

I worked awhile. Alone in the Book Nook, except for Mac, with people coming and going around me. When the introduction was finished I played through the whole thing from start to finish.

I looked up. "What does it sound like, Mac?"

Mac's big foot patted out the rhythm and he started drooling again, a sure sign of intense cerebration. "Sounds like a whore in church," he said finally. "Chantin' . . ."

"Gotta chant part all right," I said. "Colored mammy, washin' clothes. Big stack of dirty clothes . . ."

"That's it," Mac said. "Got the dirty clothes blues."

"Got the washboard blues," I said. "Rubbin' 'em up and down."

All that day I played it. Again and again. I could think of nothing else.

Harry Hostetter came in. I played it for him. He

stood there and listened, his eyes half closed, his face expressionless.

"Once more," he said, but his voice betrayed nothing.

I played it again.

He looked at me. "Hoagy," he said, "they say ashes to ashes and dust to dust—but maybe you fooled them. Maybe that one won't burn out."

Harry's attitude toward me, in some ways, was that of a tolerant father. He lived music and yet he didn't play himself. Its expression was in the work of others, me in particular, for if I showed signs of inertia he was there to goad me into working.

I remember once he said to me, "Hoagy, I've spent a lot of time on you. Don't piddle *your* time away, because you're wasting all the time *I* spent on you, too."

If I played listlessly, badly, it hurt Harry. Really truly hurt him, he loved music, loved me, and I could hurt him. Harry the tough guy, ex-Navy, been a lot of places, seen a lot of things, but it hurt him to hear me play badly.

And now I was anxious to look at my song. Stand away from it and look through the window at my creation. I got the chance a few weeks later.

Curt Hitch and His Happy Harmonists, a band from Evansville that played Wolverine style, were in town to play a dance and they heard the tune. Curt said they were going to make some records for Gennett and he wanted me to fix up another tune for him and he would record *Washboard Blues*. He needed a fast one, a hotsy number, too, so I worked out another as best I could to his specifications.

We named the new tune *Boneyard Shuffle* as a sequel to *Riverboat Shuffle* and with these two tunes we lit out for Richmond, Indiana, and the Gennett recording studios.

I was plenty nervous in anticipation of this my first recording and the studio, a dreary-looking place with horns sticking oddly from the walls, didn't have the effect of soothing me. But, still, it was a magic spot, too. It was a station on the highroad. Here one's efforts were given permanence—at least they were put on wax.

But the horns sticking from the walls looked spooky and I was pretty upset by the time we were ready to make test records.

We ran through the tunes for the technician. He, like everyone else except Harry, picked *Boneyard Shuffle* as the best number. Mainly, I think, because *Boneyard* was a hotsy-totsy number and everything had to be hot in those days—at least we all thought it did. In fact, the technician was very dubious about using *Washboard* at all, and when he found, in timing it, it was twenty seconds too short he was ready to toss it out entirely.

Just twenty seconds. The time it takes you to let your eyes drift away from these lines and light a cigarette. Twenty little beats of your pulse. I didn't realize my future hung on those twenty seconds but I felt then that my life did.

"He'll put in a piano solo," Curt told the technician.

Oh, he would, would he? Sure, Hoagy'll put in a piano solo for you. Hasn't got time to run down to the corner and buy one. He'll make one for you here. He makes three or four every morning before breakfast. Nothing to it.

I looked at him and felt whiteness around my mouth. "I can't make up a piano solo part," I said, then suddenly added, "with you mugs standing around breathing down my neck. Go out for a minute."

They left tactfully. I was left with the piano. And I tried to think of a piano solo. Instead I thought of my mother, I thought of my little sister's funeral, my mother playing hymns on the old golden oak. I thought of Monk, I thought of Larry—"ashes to ashes"—I thought of Wad —"our music's sick . . ." I thought of Bix—"I am not a swan."

I thought of everything, like the drowning man going down for the classic thrice, my fingers number on the keys, my mind going around, time running out on me. Scared, worried. And then I hit the keys.

Five minutes later I called the boys back in, the technician gave the signal and we were making a record.

Harry Wright started the introduction on the clarinet. I can see him now, standing there and blowing those plaintive notes; so young, so new to this business. He could hardly hold the reed in his mouth, and I'll never know why you couldn't hear our knees knocking together on the record. Maybe they shook in rhythm.

The cornet was taking it easy, saving his lip for the lead parts, and the piece went along.

Then it was time for the piano solo. What had I picked out while the boys were out of the room? Would I be able to repeat it? If I could repeat it, what was it? My hands were damp when I hit the keys, getting into the start of something, somehow. And then it was done. I was entirely unconscious of what I had played. We staggered through the last chorus. It was finished.

The technician, obviously still unimpressed, said he was going to play it back. "You can hear it now," he said, "and make any changes." We looked at him. Make changes. What changes? How could we change it?

Hot, quiet, breathless—and then we were hearing ourselves play.

It all sounded strange. I tried hard to believe I was hearing *my* piece, *my Washboard Blues*, but it was difficult.

And then, suddenly, the tune caught me! And came my piano solo. I didn't recognize a note of it. The record stopped.

There was a war whoop. We danced around the studio, berserk. We weren't "lukewarm and buskirk," but red-hot and berserk. The record, we thought, was terrific.

Now, as an aside, I'd like to add a note here. You as a reader, if you have an interest in music of that sort, might have recognized the piano solo that I didn't recognize. And the reason you might is because I took the theme of that piano solo, a few years later, and built it into a song and a guy named Johnny Mercer wrote a swell lyric for it and we called it *Lazy Bones*.

We didn't change *Washboard*.

Harry Hostetter got a copy of the record and he wrapped it in an old shirt and kind of gentle like took it out and laid it in our car. And a few days later he took it down to a stonecutter in Bedford, Indiana, named Fred Callahan, a friend of his, and Fred he played the record a couple of times and he laid down his chisel and took up a pen and he wrote a lyric for it about an old colored woman scrubbin' clothes. And he did a beautiful job.

Through this piece I met Paul Whiteman, made a record of it with him, and established myself, to a small degree, as a composer.

Grandpa Robison, with whom I was still staying in Bloomington, was getting along in years and his memory played tricks on him. I thought hard, trying to think of something to take back to him. Something that he would like and use. As I looked him over in my mind's eye I remembered his hat. It was a beaten-up object, of a nondescript color, originally black, and frayed here and there.

So I bought Pa a hat. It was a right snazzy number, not too conspicuous, and of a gray complexion, and expensive. I carefully withheld this gift until Sunday morning when Pa, in his best, sallied forth. I pulled out the surprise and set it on his brow at a jaunty angle. He thanked me profusely and I led him to a mirror for inspection.

Pa looked at himself with obvious approval for some seconds. "Hoagland," he said, turning finally to me, "I look purty good this morning. Just right except for this God-durned hat I got on. Remind me to get another."

In December, I took down with the flu at Ma Robison's. Dorothy Kelly was coming to see me. Lying there in bed, my bones aching, I felt ashamed, trying to cringe down into the bed to nothingness. I hated for Dorothy to see me looking like that, but she looked wonderful.

And her visit cheered me because in a couple of days I was up and soon away. So Ma Robison asked Dorothy to dinner. A dinner for us to be topped off by Ma's justly famous apple pie.

It was a fine dinner, a wonderful dinner, and Dorothy was a vision of sheer loveliness. It was a cold and blustery night outside but within it was warm. It was a night of closeness, and warmth, and when the Bloomington power plant providentially failed and Ma stood two candles on the table in the little china candlesticks, Dorothy was a picture to take your breath.

She took mine, and there was nothing I could say. After dinner we took the candlesticks to the piano and I played a little piece. "This is ours," I said huskily. "Nobody has ever heard it but us, and nobody ever will."

She thanked me and I kissed her.

Then, "Let's go down to the beech tree," I said.

Her eyes were shining, and although it was cold and windy, she nodded.

"We'll finish the initials. We'll carve them in there deep and forever." Gone were the misgivings of the other time. Gone were the doubts W's humdrum life had inspired in me, and stopped my hand that other time.

We went into the night, gay, but shaken too, by the solemnity of the occasion. Dorothy climbed into the Open Job. I turned the crank.

Nothing happened.

I turned again, more frantically. The Open Job, faithful through the years, was mute.

Does a man's life course turn on the whims of a decrepit Ford? The Open Job balked sulkily and to this day the initials are not there.

You couldn't be mean and petty and blow stuff like Bix blew. You couldn't be stupid and mundane and write stuff like Monk wrote. That's the way it is. And the things I did and the people I knew and loved are reflected in the tunes I was to write.

And if you write blues you gotta feel kinda blue sometimes.

Like when I sold the Open Job. I sold her. Sold her down the river, cut off from her parents and sold her. Of course the lads who bought her, they promised a good home, humane treatment, and I got their ten dollars and their vow that they'd be true to her.

But they were rascals, Simon Legrees in Oxford bags. They rolled her up to the curb when she sulked once under the strange hand and left her standing there, standing in the rain, inert, hurt to the depths of her differential.

I found her there, alone, cold, wet. Her radiator drooped in hopeless shame. I patted her a couple of times, whispered in her carburetor that I'd been kind, never had wisecracks painted on her; that I had come to take her home. I caressed her gas and spark, I fondled her choke. I gave her the old quarter turn and she roared to appreciative life. I was headed for Indianapolis, so I tuned up the Open Job once more and sold her again.

It was nearing the Christmas holidays. Bix blew into Indianapolis and asked me to go down to Richmond with him to hear him make some records. He phoned me at my house and I hurried down to pick him up, in my new Ford, a Christmas present to myself.

When I found him he told me that he was on his way to make some records for Gennett, the same outfit that had made our record in the fall. I was delighted to go.

Remembering my own nerve-racking experience, I thought it would be doubly pleasant to be there with no worries of my own. I asked Bix who was going to be with him on the date.

"We're going to make some records in 'slow-drag' style," Bix said, "and I've got some guys who can really go. Tommy Dorsey, Howdy Quicksel, Don Murray, Paul Mertz and Tommy Gargano. They are going to drive down from Detroit and meet me."

"Boy," I exclaimed, "that's really gonna be somethin'. What are you gonna make?"

"Hell, I don't know. Just make some up, I guess."

"How about me driving you over tonight?"

"That'll be swell," Bix said. "The guys are bringing three quarts . . ."

"When do we leave?"

"Oh, three or four," Bix said, the idea of sleeping never entering his head. He looked at a clock that showed midnight. "Let's go over to the Ohio Theatre and jam awhile."

"Now you're talkin' . . ."

We got to the theater after closing and took our places at the grand pianos in the pit. There, all alone, we banged out chorus after chorus of *Royal Garden Blues*. And each interpretation was hotter than the one before. First one of us would play the bass chords while the other played hot licks and then we'd reverse the process. When we finally wore out it was time to leave.

We started for Richmond. And that night I reached greatness.

Bix is dead now, and you'll have to take my word for it, but on that night I hit the peak. We were halfway to Richmond, of a cold dark morning, when we stopped and for some reason Bix took out his horn.

He cut loose with a blast to warn the farmers and to start the dogs howling and I remembered that my own horn, long unused, was lying in the back of the car. I got it out.

Solemnly we exchanged A's.

"Way Down Yonder in New Orleans," Bix said.

He had hit one I knew pretty well and I was in my glory.

And then Bix was off. Clean wonderful banners of melody filled the air, carved the countryside. Split the still night. The trees and the ground and the sky made the tones so right.

I battled along to keep up a rhythmic lead while Bix laid it out for the tillers of the soil. He finally finished in one great blast of pyrotechnic improvisation, then took his horn down from his mouth.

"Hoagy," he said thoughtfully, "you weren't bad."

I had achieved greatness. We drove on into the night.

We got to the studio and sat around a while and the bottles got lighter and finally Bix started doodling on his horn. Finally he seemed to find a strain that suited him but by that time everybody had taken a hand in composing the melody, though as the bottles got still lighter nobody seemed to have a definite understanding of what that melody was.

I have a photo of that group on that day. Bix is leaning against the piano, his legs crossed, and you see him in half profile. He looks so young, like a little boy, like Little Boy Blue—and he blew. Tommy Dorsey, beside him, bespectacled even at that early age is slumped in a chair, his trombone at his mouth. The rest of them are in various negligent poses, waiting.

As far as I could see they didn't have any arrangement worked out, or tune either for that matter, but when the technician came in and gave them the high sign, they took off. Away they went. Away down . . .

They named the piece *Davenport Blues* in honor of Bix's home town. It was done in lazy "jig style" and as the dead soldiers were racked up their music grew screwier and screwier.

Toddlin' Blues was the next number and by the time it was finished they were having a little trouble staying in front of their horns. But the effect was wonderful. They used the "I'se a-comin' " strain from *Old Black Joe* and there were among them those who were soon "a-comin'." A few years later three of those six boys who got together to blow jazz were gone. Little Joes, all.

But where are you going, Hoagland? Hot jazz, hot trumpet, music, blues, stomps. . . . Get that stuff out of your system, Hoagland. The law, boy, the law. That's where there is security and position. That's how Mr. Big gets to belong to the country club and play golf in the afternoon. Gets to be a person you read about in Current Events.

Might get read about in *Current Events* other ways too. Be in the back of the book, though. Under "Minds Snap Under Student Stress." Like one night it was raining—a perfect night for studies, but I just couldn't have at them. With my green slicker on and an old felt hat pulled well down in front, I braved the storm that was passing to the east. Lightning still flashed, occasionally, over the tops of the big maples.

Nowhere to go but the Book Nook. In a bad mood. A lone wolf in the dark. I step toward the door of the Nook and see that it is fairly crowded—people held indoors by the storm. Monk and Eddie Wolf, a new enthusiastic member of the Bent Eagles, were in their customary places. Perhaps the air was still electric. Maybe my entrance aroused attention. No one had entered for some time. Or maybe the hat did it. I seldom wore a felt, but at any rate I sensed that all eyes focused on me as I silently entered. One hand was thrust deep in a coat pocket. The setting was perfect and I was seized with an irresistible impulse to put on an act—an act that fit my mood.

Lowering my eyes to hatbrim level, I slowly looked straight at Monk and then from one group to another. I leveled on one or two groups and twice I quickly shifted my glance back to Monk.

"Don't move, anyone. I have a revolver!"

These well-chosen words came forth in the hollow tones of the dry-mouthed killer and the suspense was terrific. Slowly I made the complete circuit of the booths, throwing cold, glassy stares at the occupants. There was a deadly hush—a Bent Eagle gone berserk! Finally, I was back at the counter where stacks of dishes attracted my eye. Without looking at the smallest stack, I reached out my hand and gently pushed it into the sink below where the dishes made a hell of a racket. The crowd gasped for breath. Then I moved to the big stack and pushed it to the thin edge of destruction. A couple entered and I wheeled around.

"SIT DOWN! AND—DON'T MOVE!"

They did, and without a word. Then Pete Costas,

the Greek, moved in my direction. A motion of my hand in the coat pocket stopped him cold. Meekly, he pleaded with me:

"Don't do it, Hoagy, they're expensive."

I looked him squarely in the eye and gave the dishes one more perilous shove. The tension was awful and at that moment I pushed my hat back, walked quickly toward the door and said, "I think I'll go up and study."

Monk and Eddie screamed their delight and the banshee howls of relief were still audible as I crossed Fourth Street on my way home. A big hunk of ham had come out in me and I was very pleased with myself.

Next day, the story was spread far and wide that the Book Nook had been demolished the night before, single-handed, by an unknown hoodlum. People drove by in their cars and stopped to inspect the damage.

The years have pants. Striped pants and a morning coat. School pants now. But striped pants someday. Hurry, day!

And so it is the spring of '25 and I am peddling dance programs to help the kitty along, but mostly I am at the books. Torts and Contracts. Briefs and Pleadings. The law, and through the law, position. . . . That's where *I'm* going.

"Except perhaps in spring . . ." In spring a young man's fancy turneth from the law and sometimes toward home brew.

And so that spring, Harry and I spent some of our afternoons out at Granny Campbell's. Granny was an old Negro mammy who had a sure touch with the malt and the hops and the yeast that went into the dark-brown potent home brew that she dispensed.

But Granny had a misery; a misery or two and she used to sit in her old rocker and asked to be handed her own bottle. That old rockin' chair had her. Cane by her side.

"Mr. Hoagland," she told me one afternoon, "I got myself arrested once for a makin' this brew, an' I want to ast you—you is a-studyin' for the law—is makin' this good brew a *sin?*"

I laughed, but my mind was far from her question. Because in my mind were other questions. What about that phrase? Law got you so bad, so bad, you couldn't try a little tune? Little bitty old tune? Ain't that wonderful? "Old rockin' chair's got me, cane by my side . . . hand me down that . . ." Not bottle, what's the word? I got the tune, part of the tune, it's running through my head, running through my head . . . "hand me down that gin, boy, 'fore I tan yo hide . . ."

It hit me and I stuck my head up out of the water and saw Pink Cadou frolicking and splashing about. "I got it!" I yelled.

"Shhhh . . ." Harry shushed, "they'll put us under the jug forever if they catch us.

"But I got a song . . . part of a song!"

"Then let's get the hell out of here," Harry said, "or it'll be ninety-nine years in the big house."

"Mr. Hoagland," Pink Cadou said, sticking his head out of the water, "is this a sin?"

It is, as a matter of fact, a rather serious offense to swim in the reservoir and if the good folk of Bloomington tasted anything peculiar in their water it was just we-uns.

And we did get incarcerated that night, for driving negligently out Fourth Street toward the Rose Hill Cemetery. I forget what we wanted in the cemetery.

The desk sergeant said, "How do you spell your name?"

"C-a-r Michael," I told him, "anybody ought to be able to spell that."

"My God," Cadou said over my shoulder, "wait until he comes to mine."

"Why, Mr. Cadou," Harry said, "what are *you* doing here?"

"Don't you remember me? I helped you drive negligently."

"I thought Mr. C-a-r Michael was driving . . ."

"Was that a *sin?*" Pink asked plaintively, as we were ushered into cells.

"I wonder if you can get room service . . ."

But I got the song. Old Granny Campbell had plied us well that night and as the sun came over the campus Tom Huff, of the poolroom, came over the hill and bailed us out.

Pink, who had graduated the year before and had stopped by to see how things were, thanked us formally for a lovely evening. "I'm glad things haven't changed," he added.

Old Rockin' Chair, she didn't rock right away, but later when I wanted it the song was there. It came right out.

Our band held full sway on the campus through its third and last glorious year. A young town boy, with a heart that was scheduled to stop at any moment, asked us for a job tooting the bass horn. He had a clean collar and had owned the horn a month, so we gave him serious consideration. He had a fine natural ear for music and when he flattered us by demonstrating he had memorized all of our arrangements we signed him up.

We rehearsed four hours to see if he'd drop dead and when he didn't we thanked him and dealt him in for keeps. Pumping a bass horn must have been good for him, for years later he was still working on the same horn and his heart was all right.

The first dance we played that year was a great success and we gathered àt the Book Nook to congratulate ourselves.

"Hear about Charlie Robertson?" someone asked.

"You mean the guy that goes to Chicago with a saved up bankroll and registers in as visiting royalty?"

"Yeah. He played piano tonight over at another dance."

"What did he pull?"

"Came in forty minutes late, everybody waiting for him; had on white tie and clawhammer, white gloves, opera hat. He minces up to the piano, pulls off his gloves one finger at a time, puts his hat and cane down carefully, and nods superciliously to the boys. Then in a voice, utterly aloof, he announces, '*Tiger Rag,* gentlemen.' "

It was a good year, with only a few bad moments. A good year, but drawing to a close. A month after Christmas I'd be, barring accidents, a Bachelor of Latin Law. Well, at least I'd be a bachelor.

I'd be a big boy then. No more jazz, no more swimming in the waterworks, no more beer at Granny Campbell's. I'd be out in the world. The things of adolescence would be of the past. However, the future looked rosy. I had a letter from Stu Gorrell, one of the good friends and sitters, from way down in Florida:

Friday or Saturday or both.

Dear Grandfather:

Miami, the Magic City, the land of palms, the insane metropolis, is the unblemished nuts. Real estate is selling at a million dollars a spadeful, and living quarters are very seldom. Bran is thirty-five cents a bowl, but Miami, the Magic City, the land of palms, the insane metropolis, is wondering what it's all about, and so am I.

It's warm and swimmy here and you must come down, but not with a band. Night clubs are filled with wind-jammers and you wouldn't stand a chance. Acts are the rage; naked girls and wabbly choruses that would be boo-ed off a legitimate stage, are eating three times a day and getting fat.

Great personalities thrive because of their past, and new ones because of their wise schemings of the moment. Everybody has their heads together, but they are all for themselves. Come on down. I'll be standing on a corner waiting for you. I look like an old man with egg on his pants flap and a green collar-button stain on his neck. I'll be picking my teeth with a match and reading a piece of last week's newspaper.

I'm crazy about the letter X. Say it eleven times; it sounds like a little colored boy scratching his behind with a piece of cocoanut shell.

Now, you stay right here, and I'll be right back.

Yours,
Mr. Thatcher.

My own family (along with everybody else in Indiana, it seemed) had moved to Florida. I was anxious to join them and hang out a shingle.

Hoagland Carmichael, Atty. . . . Looks good, son.

Men . . . . Men . . . . . . Men
　　　　Men hanging on grapevines
Men with brooms in their ears
　　　　Shaving long rows of hogs
Men laughing like umbrellas
　　　　Over long lost underwear
But alas the rain
　　　　Has covered everything with mud
And neither hogs nor men will laugh no more.
　　　　(The author—Wolfgang Beethoven Bunkhaus
　　　　—was obliged to omit three stanzas of the above
　　　　work because he could not spell the word *Fido*)

Men, no longer boys, out in the cold, cold world.
H. Carmichael, Atty. Hogshaving by the week or month.
Remember that letter you and Harry wrote applying for
a job once? You might use part of it, circularize the town
and get some clients.

　　　. . . I would like to handle your case. I once shook
hands with an Indian and I'm a close friend of the
Spanish-American War. I haven't any experience but
my mother has. . . . She used to comb my hair and
pass me the potatoes. I studied Blooters and represented a line of hog farms, frog arms, iron dogs, fog-
horns and frog ponds. Since then I haven't been six
years old.

　　　　　　　　　　　　　Yours Respectfully,
　　　　　　　　　　　　　H. Carmichael, Atty.

P.S.　　I have a dog named
　　　　Fred.

*But, Hoagland, you got to get away from that stuff,
honest, fellow, you got to quit that. You are liable to need
a lawyer yourself if you don't leave that stuff alone.*

And time was marching. Time for my graduation, midterms of 1926. I'd had some fine years there. Wonderful years. Friendships with my fraternity brothers that would last as long as life itself. Cookie was also down in Florida. I was going to him. Pink Cadou, Granny Keller, Jack Bell, oh, all of them. Gentlemen from Indiana.

And the band, most certainly the band.

The band; I could capture a little of that to take with me. As a farewell gesture I arranged with Gennett to record a couple of tunes. Two tunes with my band— for posterity.

"What are you goin' to make?" Monk asked me in the Book Nook one day just before the term was over.

"Watch Your Hornin',"

"Hoagy," Monk said finally, "you are making a mistake."

"Why?"

"Well," he said, his voice serious, "if you remember your band, all your life you'll think it was wonderful. If you have a record of it you may play the record someday and think you weren't so good."

"But, Monk, we're the best . . . at least around here."

"Oh, sure," Monk said. "But of course. But you might not sound the best someday."

"What about the stuff you write?" I asked accusingly.

"I don't keep it," he said. "I write it to, to get it out of me . . . No matter why I write it, but I won't keep it. I won't read it ten years from now."

I thought about that conversation after we had made the records. It was Gennett's first use of the new electric equipment and the record wasn't too clear, though it sounded great to us. And maybe not so good, but tears came to our eyes as we listened to it.

Tears of affection for each other, tears at the imagined beauty of our playing. Every note an individual thing; a part of the man who played it and that man a friend. And to think that before we could get our hands on a single pressing, the master record was destroyed because of technical imperfections. Three years of friendship melted into a blob of copper.

I was leaving the next morning for Florida. I remembered what Monk said and I wondered. But Monk was wrong. We "were the best," as Wad said. I know each one of us put his heart into that record and it must have been good and true.

That record plays itself in my memory and I can hear it clearly. Wad never better on his saxophone, Chet Decker's immutable inspiring rhythm on his drums. Billy Little over his head, and that is pretty wonderful. Art Baker's handsome face creased in concentration, his lip creased into his horn, thinking Bix, as he pushed the little valves down. Harold George with the big horn and the bad heart—wasn't anything wrong with his heart that day—nor the horn, no, indeed. Bridge Abrams of the happy face bowing his fiddle like an octopus. And me, I tried hard, and there was a good deal of piano in there for a little guy.

But Monk had written me a story. A story to cheer, filled with hope and promise for me to remember in the dark days that might follow. Dark days have followed, bright days too. Good days and bad days, and the story I

have with me, in my head, to use on those days that are
dark.

Silo McRunt, Age Thirteen

Once upon a time, during an extra horse, Silo
McRunt, age thirteen, tried to count up to his mother.
His actions were noticed by his wet neighbor (a mere
bacon fanner by trade) who had just defeated his breakfast. He rushed to the phone and called Vacant 780-W,
which is the number of the Hard Lard Connecting
Works. Frantically he described the situation to Mrs.
Razzbushel, author of "The Veto of Lard Harness," or
the "Hard Varnish of Leto." Mrs. Razzbushel had been
suffering with bundles for three days, but she poured
herself into the hearse and drove at neckbreaking speed
to the scene of little McRunt, age thirteen, counting
up to his mother.

She sped through the night like a damp sausage. She
had a ham in her hand and the blisters on her feet sang
like turkey in the twilight. Meanwhile, and unknown
to her, an old man sat down in his grave.

II

We must return to the scene of little Silo McRunt,
age thirteen, counting up to his mother.

"Have you ever stink like Bozo?" he cried, falling
on his bargain.

McRunt, of course, was what one would ordinarily
McRunt. And, why not McRunt? Others had often
McRunt. From the wooded hills and templed valleys
came the soft sweet echo—"McRunt." In the North-
west, the people adopted a slogan—"Fifty-four Mc-
Runt or forty." Even in far-off Europe the feeling prevailed. Swarms of Germans filled the public squares
singing, "McRunt Uber Alles." In Local, Idaho, a man
died near a gymnasium covered with McRunt. Even
old horses sweat like McRunt.

The wet neighbor was confronted with a desperate situation. He stretched his ears for a sound of Mrs. Razzbushel. He was rewarded with his wife's belch, near the cistern. She belched again, nearer the cistern. "Ain't gravy windy?" she chortled, and with a final blast she tiptoed into the cabbage.

McRunt had won.

And I, too, had won. Ah, yes, won a law degree. A Latin Bachelor, that's me. In the law. That's where the green grass grows.

I crossed the Indiana state line in a drizzling rain to match my mood. I sped through the night like a damp sausage, like Mrs. Razzbushel. What fun I'd had, what a great gang I'd known. Thanks to Monk it was a help.

Snowbound in Pennsylvania I remembered parts of Monk's play: "The Building of the Wedding Hen." Enter: Balloon Ascension—rest of play performed in a small cave in Kokomo. Enter: Paperhangers shouting "Hen-diana, t-hen, Wiscons-hen, not-hen!" Third paperhanger: "Give these to mother." . . . Takes off trousers, dies. The end.

Yes, it was the end—I put madness to my left hand, jazz to my right hand, the two behind me forever. Amen.

PART THREE

I parked my car the next day to eat lunch and I got myself a client. Just like that. H. Carmichael, client. H. Carmichael representing the defendant. H. Carmichael, defendant.

A seedy-looking bum with a deputy's badge put the arm on me for driving without licenses to conform with West Virginia law. He took me before a dirty-faced, unshaved individual who allowed as how he was the justice of the peace and he fined me sixteen dollars and had the guts to divide it with the deputy right before my eyes. My academic knowledge of the law stood me in great stead all right, all right. I rushed out of West Virginia with all haste.

Quite a trip, that. I got stalled in a snowdrift the next morning just outside Uniontown, Pennsylvania. Natives said it was the first time in history anyone got stalled by snow on the Lincoln Highway. They pulled me out of a drift eight feet deep.

But I finally got to Washington and found my old pal, Hank Wells, deep in the business world. So deep it took us ten minutes to find a piano and have a jam session. I had put jazz behind me, forever, two days before.

"A man has to kind of wean himself," Hank said. "Taper off."

I left Hank and went on up to New York to see Irving Mills about publishing *Washboard Blues*. The record business was booming and the sheet music market was ripe for the kind of stuff I was doing. Irving offered me a job in his publishing house so I could make records and compose.

Not Hoagland. Too smart! Besides, New York didn't look wholesome to me. No trees, no leisure. "A nice place to visit but . . ."

The night before I left, Batty De Marcus and Johnny Johnson threw a party for me in the Club Mirador. Red Nichols was there, among others, to show me the "eastern style" of jazz, while I attempted to demonstrate what the boys in the sticks were doing.

George Murphy, the actor, was there that night (his was a dance act) and years later he tried to tell me, between gales of disrespectful laughter, the impression I created sartorially.

"That coat," he said. That is usually as far as he got. It seems the memory of the coat breaks him up. Actually, there was nothing wrong with the coat whatever. True, it was a coonskin, perhaps of somewhat radical design and tone, but it wouldn't cause a lifted eyebrow in Bloomington. And what the hell, what if the sleeves did catch in the keys, causing me to skip a beat. Gave the hot lick a new twist.

By three o'clock we were exhausted, and George told us a funny story.

"Tell about that job you had, Hoag. You know, the one at the meat-packing plant."

Tired and sleepy, I tried to slough it off but George

would have none of it. Red Nichols was eager to listen, so I retold it for the umteenth time.

"It was in 1918 in Indianapolis and I needed a job. The papers said that Kingan's Meat Packing Plant needed help, so I put on corduroys and a pair of high-top boots—good tops but no soles—and lined up at seven A.M. with seventy-five other job seekers. A big burly wop in a fur-trimmed coat paraded up and down like Prince Ubaldo inspecting cattle. He didn't look at me, he only looked at my boots and with a quick point of the finger I had been singled out for a job.

"A fellow took me through acres of smelly departments and we arrived at the deep end, down where the walls of the plant drop into White River. There was a half inch of cold water on the floor and the only windows were high up and barred. I had a feeling that I didn't want my instructor to leave me. It was a lonely dungeon. He took me to a metal trough through which water flowed at a lively rate, and hanging from the ceiling over the trough was a half-inch water spout, also flowing at a good clip.

" 'Here they come,' he said.

"I looked up the trough and several strange blobs of meat were headed our way. With an expert flip of the wrist he grabbed the first one by the hilt.

" 'Watch, now.'

"In a flash he jabbed the fatty hunk of meat up the water spout. There was a splash at first. And a strange odorous spray greeted our faces and hands. Then I noticed there was a tail to this horrible object. It was an entrail and the water was cleansing it of all refuse. A neat job."

" 'That's all. You take over. Get 'em all.' "

George couldn't wait to prompt me. "What were they?"

"Gentlemen," I said, as I moved toward the door, "those were pigs' asses."

George was rocking. "How long did you work at it?" He was yelling because I was starting up the steps.

"Three weeks!" And I could hear George finishing the tale.

"He had to quit because they wouldn't let him ride home on the streetcar."

They, too, had urged me to stay in New York, coat and all, but it was not for me. I was going to Florida.

The West Palm Beach that I reached was hardly recognizable. It had grown tenfold since 1922 and what had been a quiet resort was now a mad boom town.

As Stu Gorrell had said, everyone was for himself, scheming to get his picture on a silver dollar. Prices were sky high. Cookie and I moved into a small basement apartment and I hung out a shingle, so to speak.

Cookie was a fine lawyer and my constant association with him rubbed off some of his legal knowledge onto me and things went along first rate.

Music seldom entered my head. I played piano occasionally in a café where we dined, smug in my knowledge that I wasn't one of the many jazz hounds stranded in Palm Beach and Miami when the bubble burst.

I was reminded of my good fortune again when Taz Walters (of the braces) and Jimmy Hartwell, of the Wolverines, blew into town. Taz had a pawn ticket and a tale of woe.

Jimmy had hocked the watch—Taz's watch—to have

a photographic portrait made of himself. He looked well in the pose and the loss of the watch didn't make Taz too unhappy. It didn't make Jimmy Hartwell remorseful either. It seemed normal, it was fun. They were going to play a job—a ten-day triangle cruise between West Palm Beach, Havana and Miami and things would be all right. I felt a twinge of envy for them.

Something went wrong. Taz couldn't make the cruise. It took me ten minutes to find Vic Moore over at Bradley's Casino and borrow his drums and sign myself on as the drummer. No, Vic wasn't using them. He had gone social on us and was gambling some dame's money.

I put up a fair bluff as a drummer, though I'd never played drums before in my life, and I played the piano in the afternoon while the captain sipped tea with the ladies. And then we arrived in Havana.

One Night in Havana. I wrote that tune the first night I came home from the cruise, but I put in three days and nights gathering material for it . . . and if I do say so, I was thorough. No, you've never heard it. It wasn't published.

Tropical nights, tropical beer, tropical music, tropical girls, tropical moon, tropical mood. Yes, indeed.

"Hello," she said in faintly exotic accents.

"Hello," I said in faint Indiana accents, making an alley down the empty beer bottles, better to survey this vision.

She sat down.

"Drink?" I asked gallantly.

She agreed.

Now, the Havana B-girl functions much like her sorority sisters elsewhere in the world. Each drink she had, and each drink I had, gave her a ticket or a chit which she turned in for her percentage at the end of the evening. However, her exotic beauty blurred my repugnance to the somewhat sordid undertone this gave our relationship. In fact, I was a first-class blur all around. She seemed strangely blonde and danced divinely. The beer was strong. The rumba music, the first I had heard, gave me a tingle like the first time I had heard Chicago jazz. The drummers, Jamaicans usually, were really good. They hit a tantalizing beat.

My companion led me to realize I was a fascinating tycoon from the Colossus of the North. And I was pretty colossal. Truly, a night of romance; a night to remember.

"Where are you from, darling?"

"Pierre," she told me in that fascinating unplaceable accent.

I didn't place Pierre. Obviously, though, this sloe-eyed señorita was part French. And weren't the French supposed to be leading the league in l'amour? Ah, yes, indeed, Hoagy, you Don Juan of the Carribean.

We were dancing and she melted into my arms a touch more intimately and I executed a few more versions of my rumba—à la Student Building, Bloomington—and she followed every step.

"Pierre," I murmured.

"Yes," she said. "Pierre, South Dakota."

Somehow that chilled my passion, but still it was a wonderful cruise and I wrote a rumba.

But, like the señorita from Dakota, there was something wrong with the law, now. It seemed to become duller and more prosaic in my absence.

"Cookie," I said one day in the office, "we're doin' all right, aren't we?"

Cookie looked at me and smiled. "Sure," he said, but there was something almost like pity in his voice. "Sure, Hoagy."

"Cookie, it looks like . . ." But I didn't finish the sentence. "What's that?" I yelled.

For coming to my ears was a sound. The sound of music, a haunting refrain. It flooded my mind with memories, with hopes and desires a thousand times stronger than any others I had ever known or would ever know.

For, across the street an unknown hand had changed my destiny forever. That hand had placed on a phonograph a round black record and had dropped a needle gently on it. That and nothing more.

I jumped up, stood there. "That's *Washboard Blues*," I hollered. *"MY Washboard . . ."* I ran out of the office and I heard Cookie's steps behind me.

It was coming to me as I ran, clearly and wonderfully; and it was mine.

We got to the music store, stood there a moment watching the record go around, trying to read the name on it. Finally it stopped. It was a record that I hadn't known had been made. Red Nichols had made it. Good old Red.

We played it again and again. Then, finally, we went slowly back across the street. I made my way to my desk aimlessly and started straightening up. I looked up at Cookie.

"Hoagy," he said, and his voice was kind and amused, "you never had a chance."

I felt a great weight go off my mind. "Maybe," I said

happily, "I can get up home in time for the Junior Prom. I hear Jean Goldkette's coming down and he's got Bix and Frank Trumbauer and Joe Venuti and . . . Hell, all the boys will be there."

Cookie grinned. "I need a vacation myself. I'll go with you."

Our preparations for this descent on Bloomington included a suitcaseful of bootleg liquor with wisps of Nassau seaweed still laced in the protective burlap sacking. We were careful to get the brand that was then being hidden, by the rumrunners, at the bottom of the Atlantic and later brought ashore.

We were going to win people and influence friends in the old home town.

We arrived for the Prom. That was a night. Bix was at his peak then, and the violent grace of Joe Venuti sawing his fiddle fascinated us. In that complicated mosaic of his music there was no hole. Endless, tireless, perfect. Solid.

Red Ingle doodling his lyrics had us in hysterics. Off-color inanities, in staccato, baffled the chaperons. "Do-dada-la, corkupbutgrabuptitandslugupashot . . ." are dimly remembered samples.

The chaperons were dizzy that evening and when the dance was over Monk composed one of his greatest lines for Bix.

One by one a cow goes by

Bix's eyes popped, he turned his head a little to the side as he did on the bandstand, when great things were coming from his horn, and murmured happily, once again, his entire vocabulary of praise and admiration. "I am not a swan."

The great days were upon me once more. Music, friends, happiness and poverty. The good life. No pleadings except to plead with Bix to "do that again" on his horn. To Monk to "say that line again."

Harry moved into our house and I started working on the piano. He would listen silently and if I caught him grinning and rubbing his hands that meant that some pretty note had caught his fancy. We listened to all the new records. Frank Trumbauer was now making recordings for Okeh and his releases were superb. Bix, Eddie Lang, and other greats played with him on these disks and when his record of *Singing the Blues* appeared, the ultimate in jazz technique was there for the boys to ponder. The record was a sensation among musicians even if the public didn't buy it. The public was interested in radio. The tree of hot jazz flourished, but the roots were slowly dying.

Of Trumbauer's records, *I'm Coming, Virginia* and *Way Down Yonder in New Orleans* were my favorites. Bix's choruses on these were a complete musical education. Add his chorus in the Okeh record of *Riverboat Shuffle* and his work on Whiteman's *Sweet Sue* and *China Boy* and you've got it all.

Paul Whiteman brought his band to the Indiana Theatre in Indianapolis and Harry and I hurried down. Bix had joined the band along with Trumbauer, the Dorsey boys, Bill Rank, Eddie Lang and Joe Venuti. Whiteman now had an orchestra that made the title "King of Jazz" rightly his.

We found Bix at the stage entrance and he introduced me to musicians I had admired for years. The Rhythm Boys—Bing Crosby, Al Reicker and Harry Barris—were there to make Whiteman's jazz panorama complete.

Bix was much bigger than when I had last seen him and he looked well, exuding an atmosphere of jovial success and prosperity, from his neat bow tie to his shiny shoes.

He had grown quite handsome and for a moment I was playing third base to him. But the feeling of remoteness vanished almost immediately when he took us in and introduced us to Whiteman himself.

The reception that Paul gave us was unfeignedly spontaneous and he put us quickly at our ease. He told us a couple of his favorite stories and then, more or less out of a clear sky, he said, "Hoagy, that Gennett record you all made of *Washboard* is a great job. It's really a good record."

I sat there trying to think of something to say without success, and then I heard Harry's voice.

"Have you heard about the lyric?"

"No."

"Well," I heard Harry begin, "there is a stonecutter down in Bedford, Indiana, and he heard the tune . . ." Harry's voice went on telling of the lyric, but I didn't hear much of what he said. Paul's words and his personality had me spellbound.

Paul took me by the arm and led me to the piano. "Okay, son, you sing it."

"But I've never sung," I stammered.

"Sing it."

With Tommy and Jimmy Dorsey at one end of the

piano and Paul and Harry at the other I did the number the best my wheezy voice would permit.

There was a long moment of silence and I stole a glance at Paul's face. It was rubicund and bland. Then he turned to his manager. "Gillette, get a ticket for this guy tomorrow. He's going to Chicago with us and sing for the concert record we're going to make of *Washboard.*"

I gulped, I almost fainted. But he laid a big, kind paw on my shoulder. "It's going to be all right," he said.

I guess he could feel me trembling, though, for suddenly he laughed to himself and said, "Did you ever hear about the time Trumbauer was a fireman on the railroad? Fired for an old guy they called Cranky Joe . . ."

He went on with the story, a wonderful story that took my mind off the ordeal of singing for a record. It seems Trumbauer went to work firing for this Cranky Joe, the toughest engineer out of East St. Louis, with a saxophone under one arm and a lunch pail under the other. And he got away with it. As a matter of fact, in a few weeks he had the engineer giving him a hand with the shovel so he could get his reeds and pads in shape so he could get to blowing when they hit the roundhouse.

At this point, Frankie himself walked in, grinned and took up the conversation.

"Ever hear about Isham Jones? He worked in a coal mine all day and played sax half the night. Now, you know you can't keep fit that way. Well, one day he falls asleep and misses setting the sprags in the rails so the coal cart won't run away. Course they was a tee-ired mule in front o' that cart. Ish wakes up just as they're about to reach the first turn and plops off. They say that mule's been looking all over the country for him ever since. That's when he beat it for Chicago and put a band in at the College Inn. Bad break!"

"Is Howdy with your band?" I ask Paul.

"He shouldn't be after last week. The curtain comes up and I'm taking a bow and the audience laughs. I look around and there's Howdy asleep on the front row. Band's getting so damn big I can't keep track of 'em all. But did I tell you about Joe Venuti in New York? Course not. We're playing a private party on Fifth Av'noo and the host—full of that stuff—comes in airy-like and says, 'Let's have some excitement, boys.' Venuti, in that guttural tone says, 'You want some excitement?' and at that he picks up the little white piano by himself and tosses it out the fourth-story window. A MAD man!"

"But Paul didn't tell you what he did to Howdy the next day." It's Jimmy Dorsey speaking.

When the curtain goes up Paul reaches for Howdy's brand-new guitar and takes a big bite out of it. You could hear it crunch up in the rafters."

The talk went on. Kind talk from people who were putting me at ease. My kind of talk. Talk of music and musicians.

Hoagy, you are a musician again. Among your kind. Talking your language. This is your world. Remember McRunt, Hoagland. Why not McRunt—others have often McRunt. Sing, McRunt!

In the Uptown Theatre in Chicago, where Paul's orchestra was playing, I stood in the wings and watched the boys go. Between shows we gathered in the small basement rooms and played hot jazz. Bix and Jimmy

Dorsey were almost always in on these sessions; it was down in these little rooms, too, that I practiced what, for lack of a better word, I will call my "singing." I had a good deal of it to do in *Washboard* (a good deal too much, I thought) and the recording date was approaching.

Bing Crosby came around while I was rehearsing once. "Let me see the words, Hoagy."

"What for?"

"I'd just like to learn it," Bing said tactfully.

"What for? I'm gonna sing it."

"Sure, but it's a swell number and I'd like to learn it."

Dumb? Well, yes. I didn't realize until later that Paul wanted some insurance. If I couldn't do it, he wanted somebody there who could. Bing was being kind. He didn't want me to know I might flop. They had a date to make a record and they wanted to make a record whether I was on it or not.

It was here that I noticed the crowds of people who flocked to the stage entrance to see Bix. These people, usually musicians, would crowd around him and urge him to play. Bix was meeting so many people it was driving him nuts. He tried faithfully to remember them all, to keep them straight in his mind and not offend anyone; but he was being idolized and it was bad for his nerves.

It seemed, too, that there was always a bottle in his room. Occasionally I would hear Paul ask, "How's Bix this afternoon?" Bix was Paul's baby and he loved him as if he had been his own little boy.

The record of *Washboard Blues* was made at the

Victor studios and *Among My Souvenirs* was recorded on the other side. I was so nervous that I ruined many master records. I had a lot of vocalizing to do and the piano solo I had done for the Gennett record was included in the arrangement. It was nerve-racking, jumping from one act to another, but we finally got a master that was approved.

Ridin' on the upbeat. Every bump in the Monon's track as light as air as we rattle through Lafayette, Crawfordsville and points south. The upbeat is wonderful when you are ridin' it steady and solid. What fun to sing on records. What a great bunch of guys the Whiteman bunch are. How very sure of themselves. Nothing corny there—a life of pure imagination and "sweet talk."

"Talk sweet, boy! Talk to yourself."

"Okay—now listen, Bub, this Hoagland fellow is through—see—he's through. Oh, yes, you can use him occasionally to sign insurance papers and affidavits, but not checks—he's through. Follow that road of pure imagination, boy. Just get in there and write those songs. That's sweet talk. That's you. And how do you do it—? *free wheeling,* son, *free wheeling.*"

In Bloomington, between the summer session and the fall term opening of the university it was quiet. The town was deserted and the Book Nook was closed. I wandered over to look in on an old friend, and early love, Kate Cameron. Perhaps I didn't go to see Kate, maybe I went to her house because there was a piano there; a piano for free wheeling.

We talked, we laughed. She was provocative. I loved

to look at her legs. Everybody admired her legs. She inspired the boys. I always wanted to play *good* for Kate. Gump Carter was there, the ever-faithful Gump like a shaggy dog. His unaffected and simple adoration of Kate had dated from his childhood and a case of scarlet fever that had left him ill equipped for the realities of life. I fooled on the piano, something bothering me. Then Kate's date arrived and Gump and I went out. We went to see Pete Costas at the Book Nook. Finally I left and Gump wandered off on one of his aimless journeys.

It was a hot night, sweet with the death of summer and the hint and promise of fall. A waiting night, a night marking time, the end of a season. The stars were bright, close to me, and the North Star hung low over the trees.

I sat down on the "spooning wall," at the edge of the campus and all the things that the town and the university and the friends I had had there flooded through my mind. Beautiful Kate, the campus queen . . . and Dorothy Kelly. But not one girl—all the girls—young and lovely. Was Dorothy the loveliest? Yes. The sweetest? Perhaps. But most of them had gone their ways. Gone as I'd gone mine.

I'd seen Dorothy off and on but it wasn't the same as in the early days. And how can I explain it? Do you love poetry better than filet mignon? Most people have room for all their loves and maybe I didn't. Perhaps music was my only real love.

I wrote to Dorothy when I was away from her and I probably waxed most lyrical in these epistles about some music I had heard. And she could read the lines all right, and between the lines all right too.

We had an understanding, vague and wordless. More

precisely we had another understanding. And that was to let the other know when and if the "blush went from the rose."

She kept that bargain, and I, years later in New York, didn't answer her last letter.

And finally she wired me she was to be married.

Never be twenty-one again; so in love gain. Never feel the things I'd felt. "The memory of love's refrain . . ."

I looked up at the sky and whistled *Stardust*.

Now excitement was upon me. I ran for Pete's piano.

"Got to use your piano, Pete."

"What for?"

"Very important . . ."

"Gotta close up." But he gave me a few minutes and the notes sounded good.

Next morning, the good smell of Pa's bacon gravy awakened me. And then I remembered. How did that melody go? Oh, yes, in B-flat. I was humming it, absorbed, under my breath at the breakfast table.

"What did you say, Hoagland?"

I looked at her and grinned, "Nothing, Ma. These are mighty fine biscuits."

The years have pants! Kansas City, and with a new Goldkette band. Andy Secrest blowing like Bix. Needled beer. Fried shrimp. Women.

"Hoagy, what is a writ of replevin?"

"Hell, I don't know. Who's that cute little girl at the end of the bandstand?"

"Don't know—but you're fired, Hoagy. The joint

can't support two piano players. Why don't you go see Don Redman on the way home?"

"I will, but who's that little girl?"

"Something they call an alley-gator or gutter-bug or something. Good luck, boy."

I found Don standing in front of the band, at the Greystone ballroom in Detroit—a short bowlegged fellow directing with a drumstick. And how his gang responded! They bowled me over. This was music with a solid beat and a rockin' rhythm, when the five-brass team cut loose. The ensemble choruses were built around phrases that smacked of the old Negro spirituals. They employed blues strains of the camp-meeting variety and then rode them to death with five brasses. The saxophone section played with the power of a steam engine.

But, in spite of this radical treatment, it wasn't all bleating blatant jazz. Don had written some fine music, and it was there for you to hear.

We got along—Don and I—first rate. He took me to the Negro speakeasies where I saw white girls with Negroes for the first time. My eyes popped and I felt ashamed. Don shrugged. "It's in bad taste," he said, "and bad taste knows no color line. But the hard-boiled eggs and beer are good. Try 'em." We stuffed and talked shop.

Next day we had dinner at his house and his beautiful wife fed us fried chicken, the like of which I cannot remember. She waited on Don as if he were a king and it occurs to me this shopworn simile is not amiss. A king Don Redman was. Before leaving I handed him a manuscript. "Just a little new tune, Don. You might want to play it." He did play it—the first to play it and a song was started on its little journey to success. Little journey?

Why, it took it three long, hard years of trouping to make the grade. From Don to Jean Goldkette and then Isham Jones was handed a lead sheet that Vic Young got from Jean. It was the hard way in those days. No radios to make a hit overnight.

Some fourteen-handicap wit once said that home is where you go when you haven't any place else to go. In a way he was right, for me at least, for I hadn't any place else to go for the things that home meant to me. I came down from Detroit and walked, unheralded, into our house.

There was my mother, playing cards with Harry; there sat the piano, the old golden oak. Love and warmth, cheer and affection. You haven't any place else to go for those.

Mother looked beautiful and Dad looked handsome. Harry still thinks I am some punkins. We talked far into the night, recalling things, the gay things and the sad things. My mother told me she took me to the fraternity dances she played on the campus when I was very little and laid me out to sleep on two collapsible chairs.

"Ragtime on the piano," she said, "were your lullabies."

"Did the girls like me?"

"Oh, they loved you, they thought you were the cutest thing."

"Ah, to be four again . . . no, it's better this way."

But Harry had got up and wandered to the piano. I looked at him in amazement as he sat down. Harry had never played anything. But painfuly, with one finger, he picked out a familiar tune.

"What's that?" I asked. It's funny how you don't recognize your own tunes sometimes. Then: "Get up, Harry, I want to hear Mom beat out *Maple Leaf Rag* and *Cannonball.*"

Mother sat down at the piano and she played those numbers as no one before or since has played them.

My dad looked at me and smiled. "She's wonderful, isn't she, son?"

I nodded agreement, my throat tight with emotion.

Harry went back to the piano and his one-finger playing.

"What *is* that? Oh, yes, now I remember."

"That's *Stardust*," Harry said. "That's the only piece I ever learned. Don't you ever forget it. But in case you should I learned it, too."

I smiled at him again. Afraid to trust my voice, I didn't tell him I had given a lead sheet of it to Don the week before. Yes, home is where you go for things that are no place else.

So I put new thought to *Stardust*. Stu Gorrell, my roommate at college, had named it. He was the one who had taught me to smoke before breakfast and this was his atonement. He came running around the Soldiers and Sailors Monument on the circle in Indianapolis one day to catch up with me. He had it.

"Call it *Stardust*," and his hands and fingers made a high-reaching gesticulation in the manner of dust falling from the sky. Where he had found it I hadn't the slightest notion and I hesitated to ask him for fear he'd tell me another of his little high-sounding fabrications. It fit and that was it.

Not content with a verse and chorus, I added a piano interlude and a passage for clarinet. Emile Seidel heard it and his gang and I made the trek to Richmond that gave it its first recording.

A ragged rendition perhaps and during the play-back I felt that the melody seemed to sustain us in spite of our playing. And then it happened—that horrible thought; that queer sensation that this melody was bigger than I. It didn't seem to be a part of me. Maybe I hadn't written it at all. It didn't sound familiar, even, and the recollection of how, when and where it all happened became vague as the lingering strains hung in the rafters of the studio. To lay my claims I wanted to shout back at it, "Maybe I didn't write you, but I found you."

Two years later, Mitchell Parrish wrote the words.

Although I did not know it at the time, Walter Winchell heard a piano rendition of the tune by a Sepian at the Black Feets Café in Greenwich Village—and he got a new kind of love, so he tells me. Contemporary newsmen were forced to put the drinks down while Walter held them by the lapels and whistled the first four bars. In this way *Stardust* became known as the Walter Winchell song. Later, after the song had waned in popularity, Edgar Hayes picked up the torch and gave the Negro population of Harlem a quiet, tinkly piano version under a moony stage and the song gathered new life. To these people and the song's many friends throughout the country I am very grateful.

One more trip to the Gennett studios with a bunch of college musicians and the big maples and I were to part forever, it seems. This time to record *March of the Hoodlums* and *Walkin' the Dog*. The little green horn and I did a solo. We listened, parted friends and I haven't

seen her to this day. I think Mother gave her to a little
boy up the street.

Roll on, sweet chariot, carryin' me to Hollywood.
Lot of Texas, awful lot of Texas, and then the colors get
the same and you are in the desert, and there's a lot of
desert too.

But everything's all right. Got an upper berth, got a
couple of good suits, got some songs under my arm.
That's where the rainbow hits the ground for composers.
Hollywood.

Come out of the desert and man has made it green.
Magic water, beautiful and green. Be there soon. Pretty
soon now. Got a new one under my arm. *Old Rockin'
Chair,* thought of that one early one morning swimming
in the Bloomington reservoir after all night drinkin' of
Granny Campbell's home brew. Got *One Night in Havana,* thought of that one dancing with a gal from South
Dakota down in Havana one night. Got *Washboard
Blues.* Beat out that one on the old Book Nook piano;
all day long I beat it out. I got *Stardust.* That one's all
the girls, the university, the family, the old golden oak,
all the good things gone, all wrapped up in a melody.

Going out to Hollywood on the Southern Pacific in
an upper berth to put my hopes and my loves and my
fears and my despairs up on a counter in the form of
songs and sell them.

"Los Angeles!"

Then Hollywood. The fabled streets of Beverly
Hills, the magic land. I was glad I'd come.

However, I seemed to be the only one that was glad.

I learned angles, but placed no songs. I tried the studios and learned I had: One, The wrong address. Two, I hadn't been sent for.

But that was all right. I didn't mind too much. Paul Whiteman and his band had come out to make "King of Jazz," but there was story trouble and the band waited out the summer having a wonderful time. I did my bit to help them. A clambake for sure. And there was tragedy too that summer.

Bix was losing his grip.

Don Murray, the boy who did the clarinet work that day at Richmond, Indiana, when Bix and his gang made *Davenport Blues,* died suddenly. It was shocking news to the whole jazz fraternity. Rapollo of the New Orleans Rhythm Kings had been placed in an insane asylum and Tommy Gargano of that day at Richmond had died a year earlier.

And now, Bix was losing his grip. Fumbling at rehearsals. He was great after that, sometimes as great as ever, but he was slipping and it hurt to realize that.

Al Reiker introduced me to his sister, Mildred Bailey, and I went often to her house to hear her sing. Sitting in a rocking chair, drinking beer and listening to her do my own number *Rockin' Chair* like nobody else was a real thrill. Louis Armstrong's latest record releases, with the beautiful trumpet passages and the gut-bucket vocals, kept our hearts pounding. Later Paul Whiteman booked Mildred on his Old Gold program and *Rockin' Chair* became her theme song.

I mentioned Bix's having moments, still, of greatness. I tell you of one night. Richard Barthelmess had a birthday party. Paul Whiteman and his band were invited. I wasn't, but I was there in hearing distance when Paul marched his band onto the stage, which had been built for him, and played *Weary River,* the theme song of Barthelmess's current picture.

And then *Rhapsody in Blue!*

That horn! Bix was in there that night all right. They all were. They were inspired. I'll never hear *Rhapsody in Blue* like that again. I hope God was listening, for there was beauty there that night.

Before the summer ended other friends showed up in Hollywood. Andy Secrest, who was giving Bix a run on the cornet, was living with me and we drank out of the same beer can. Batty De Marcus came out to learn flying. He had thrown his beautiful saxophone into the East River because playing it finally had worked loose every tooth in his head. Western Branch Order of Bent Eagles: We got out a play of Monk's and read it:

*Culps Down Feltment, Or Whose Color Is Your
Sweater Now?*

Act I

Scene:

The Mississippi. It is evening and there is a feeling of football in the river. Three old men are seated on a nervous horse.

First Old Man:

I am an old man, now. For many years I have been coming through the weather. I own a garage.

Second Old Man:

That reminds me of Minnie.

Third Old Man:

Whose horse? What Minnie?

(First old man falls off horse and drowns. He goes

down spelling sapolio—horse becomes ambitious and looks like violin)

Act II

Scene:

Market in Hthvp, Siberia. Two old men and nervous horse are measuring pears.

Enter:

Four-story building followed by several smaller stories. Man leaps from window of building and lands on nervous horse. Horse dies.

Man:

(Whose real name is Hollis Twelvecakle alias Horace Dozennoises, but better known in his home town as Leah Q. Peters) Did I hear you guys talking about Minnie?

Second Old Man:

Whose Minnie? What talking?

(Third Old Man dies of enthusiasm)

Second Old Man:

When Minnie was nine years old she got an option on a deep chicken.

Twelvecakle (sobbing on pears):

Whose chicken? What Minnie?

The End

We sat enthralled, we screamed. We had another drink.

But obviously this manner of living couldn't keep up forever and when Paul Whiteman's special train left for New York, I bummed a ride sharing a berth with Bing Crosby.

"Good thing you're scrawny," Bing told me, when I climbed in his berth that first night.

"If I'd stayed there till I got a studio job," I said, "I'd have been able to sleep in a piccolo case."

"That's picture business," he said. "It's all right, I guess, except the hours are bad. Me, I like to take it easy."

"They let me take it too *damned* easy," I said.

But Bing had gone to sleep, snoring slightly in perfect pitch to the train whistle, as we rumbled through the desert.

Awhooooooohooo. So long Hollywood, see you later.

I still didn't care deeply for New York and eyed it with distrust, but I found Stu Gorrell living in the Village with some other Indiana University boys and they gave me a cubbyhole that looked like the place succeeding generations of janitors had crawled off to die in. Later I moved to Jackson Heights where there were trees.

One night while at a friend's, Hube Hanna, my first inspiration on the piano, dropped in. But Hube wouldn't play for me. His chief interest was the Goodyear Company. The business world had swallowed up my first "king."

Bix was sick. Whiteman had sent him home and he had come back again to New York, but he hadn't rejoined Whiteman's band and that had hurt him. He was drinking pretty hard, and staying to himself in his hotel room for days at a time. His only recreations were moving pictures such as "Wings" and "Hell's Angels." He was crazy about flying; occasionally he would visit the city morgue.

Jazz was dying and the man who was its epitome was dying, too. He worked occasionally on his piano compositions. *Flashes, Candlelights, In the Dark.* Whiteman's arranger, Bill Challis, came by at times to get them on paper. Thanks to Bill, these beautiful things were preserved. The darkness was closing in on Bix and he didn't seem to care.

Only in Harlem could I find the music that I craved. Duke Ellington and Fletcher Henderson were playing in the Don Redman style, but the Duke especially was going much further. His arrangements had a color that no one else approached and he was doing jazz a real service in transforming the ugly picture some people had of it into beautiful fantasies. *Mood Indigo,* to name only one, was the product of a true genius.

I went by Bix's room one day. I met a maid in the hall. "What's the matter with that fellow, anyway?" she asked. "Who is he? He hasn't been out of his room for three days."

Funny little mouth and teeth that are none too strong . . . Pivot tooth fell out one night when he leaned out of a hotel window to yell down at me. We searched for it frantically with matches so Bix could play that night.

Tell the maid. Who is he?

Kid sitting at the piano with a phonograph beside him. Speed regulator is pushed clear back and he's memorizing each slow note as it whines off the disk.

A friend brings in a cornet. That's for him.

"Want to sell it, Fritz?"

"Sure, for enough to get a sax."

"How much?"

"Thirty-five bucks."

"I can't pay it all now." Not now or ever. He still owes Fritz nine of that thirty-five.

Tell the maid, Hoagy.

He comes back from a music lesson. He waves to

people as he walks along the street, a pale hand coming out of an old sheepskin coat sleeve. They like him. The teacher liked him too. "Tell your mother that your theories of harmony are such that you can learn nothing from me. And I mean that as a compliment, my boy."

Tell the maid, Hoagy.

But how could I? . . . *Bix and I on the floor, listening to the "Firebird." Doodling with Bix under the pavilion in Indianapolis when he was with the Wolverines. Bix blasting the night air with that incomparable horn, the night we drove to Richmond to make the records. Bix up there on the bandstand, night after night, week after week; creating, making great music, hot and lovely, every time they turned him loose. Bix, the incomparable genius, but a human being with it all, subject to the ills of the flesh, the tortures of the spirit. And no way to say it except with the horn and the horn wouldn't say it all.*

I looked at the maid's blank face. "Just a guy," I said. I went on to his room.

"Hi, Hoagy." Bix was lying on the bed. He looked bad, there was something missing, as if part of him were already "in the dark."

"Hi, Bix." I sat down. I was uneasy. "How's it goin', fellow?"

Bix smiled wanly. "What are *you* doing?"

"Been listening to the publisher's theme song: '*It's Not Commercial.*'"

Bix looked away and then I heard his voice. "Don't worry, boy. You're . . . ah, hell . . ."

"Get out your horn. Let's doodle a little."

He shook his head. "Ran into a girl the other day,"

Bix said, "she's going to fix me up in a flat out in Sunny-side."

"Swell. Get out of this dump and you'll feel better. You might eat something."

He looked at me and the veil went from his eyes for a moment. "How's for bringing her over some night?"

"Sure, any time," I said.

And Bix brought the girl and came to my apartment one night. We didn't have a drink, we didn't talk music, and it soon became apparent that this girl had no idea who Bix was. And then the terrible thought struck me— I didn't know either. He was my friend yet I didn't know him. He was the unfathomable. Perhaps she knew he was a musician, but that was all.

He went out of the room for a moment. "Listen," I said, "if Bix ever gets sick, if anything happens, *let me know*. Let me know right away!"

"All right," she said, a little wonderingly. "I'll let you know."

Bix came back. "You still with Irving Mills?" he asked.

"Yeah, I do some recording, but it's not a living. I'm working for an investment banking house, too."

"You won't quit music, Hoagy?"

"Uh-uh . . ."

"You know," he said suddenly, "I won't either. But I'm right back where I started . . . no job . . ."

"Where'd you start?"

"We got up a band, Buckley's Novelty Orchestra, and we got a job at the Terrace Gardens in Davenport. But, there was a union band there and we had to join the union. To join the union you had to read music. I didn't."

"What did you do?"

"I memorized everything cold. But cold. And we got up there and I looked at the sheet and blew right good . . . and then they double-crossed me . . . they stuck one up I hadn't learned."

"How'd you get around that?"

"Well," Bix said, "I played exactly what the piano played, right behind it. Of course, I was supposed to be playing something else and they knew it. It cost us the job. Jesus, I felt bad about that."

"Good God, what you were doing was a hell of a sight harder than reading . . ."

Bix grinned his shy grin and it lit up his face. "Well," he said, "you know I never did finger that bugle right."

Bix has a girl. Good for him. And I thought of my girl—the girl who *was* my girl. Dorothy Kelly, the "little bunch of sweetness," liked the simple things and in a slow tempo. For me, music and the ambition to live it and write it, and a life of simple domesticity could not compete.

We corresponded and as her diminishing affection for me became apparent in her letters my replies became harder to write. And finally so hard as to be impossible.

I remember the last letter I tried to write. The one I couldn't write, and then there came the wire saying that she was to be married.

Have to write that letter. Write "Dearest Dorothy" and that is all you write. It won't go down there on the paper, but there are some things you want to say because she'd understand.

When the snow falls through the maples in Bloomington all things are beautiful. The snow takes away every harsh angle and the things the snow hides are rounded, soft and immaculate. When the snow falls in New York people grind it into a dirty pulp and it is hauled away with much clatter. It doesn't matter to a guy who is in a roaring subway riding up to Harlem to hear the Duke do things no other royalty can do because he'll learn a thing or two. The guy is me and I want to write the things that the Duke will play.

"My dearest Dorothy": I must write you that letter. This letter about you and me, about the things we dreamed of . . . about a house on the hill and wistaria vines. I like wistaria. With you under it who wouldn't. But the music, I like it too. I have to have it. I have to have New York right now. It's exciting. I makes me want to be somebody. But I am still nobody. . . . I couldn't keep you here . . . the house on the hill is a fourth-floor walk-up furnished in sheet music and a Gideon Bible.

The snow melts in Bloomington and the Jordan River tumbles importantly, a real river for a little while. The sun shines and the grass turns green. There are flowers and the soft spring rains drip through the maples and the Student Building bells spill sweet music over the campus. But there is other music in that benign air . . . lovely, lyrical, but sometimes hot and urgent.

"My darling Dorothy": Last night I went to hear a five-piece band in a speakeasy on 52nd Street. You'd like it for a while but not for long. It's going to take me a long time, Dorothy, and I'll have to spend half my time in taxicabs because it is urgent. *Stardust* was written under the maples but there are others to write. And here, yes, here. So I can't think of you now nor the house on the hill. I can write what I want now because I know I won't send it to you.

The maples leaf out in Bloomington. The moon climbs over the hill and you find notes on the piano in that season you didn't know were there. You know there are others to be found—notes that can be rushed quickly to the publishers. Perhaps there is another Bix to be found and you might miss him sitting in a house on a hill. But that is a strange thing to say . . . didn't Harry Hostetter find Bix on just such a night playing to a house on a hill? Yes, indeed, at the very top of Sorority Row. But I'm a little strange now, too, and in a big strange city. I like it though, and something tells me there is a future in it.

"Dear Dorothy": I have your wire, now, finally, and I know you understand. I hope you will be happy with Art. He is a damned fine man. I remember when he got a piece of rope for Christmas. But now it's all solid with him. A good job . . . no more horn tootin'. It's better this way. The words on this yellow sheet shimmer a little because maybe my eyes are wet . . . for things that are gone and won't come back . . . and I keep telling myself that you can't love music more than a girl like you and I know that is right. But I could also be a liar the way things are, and I'll write you about that someday but I know I won't. I'm going out again tonight. Louie Armstrong is in town. He's going to show me purty notes and

I'll learn some more about composing. But you needn't care about that now. I hope that you are happy, yes, I do.

The years have pants. Mine were shiny polishing a chair in front of a desk. Bix's pants were shiny, too, and unpressed. Louis Armstrong came into New York and we made *Rockin' Chair.* Those big lips of his, at the mike in front of my face, blubbering strange cannibalistic sounds, tickled me to the marrow.

I got a band together to make *Lazy River,* a new song I had done. Did I say a band? Listen. I had Jimmy Dorsey, Tommy Dorsey, good old Jackson Teagarden, Gene Krupa, Benny Goodman, Bud Freeman, Joe Venuti, Bix (and he was right that day), and others of that caliber.

While at the Victor plant I looked up a pressing of *One Night in Havana* that Fred Waring had made some years before. The first American attempt at a rumba with gourds and sticks but the Victor Company refused to release the record. I found it in a pile of junk and marked across the face in red pencil were the inspiring words "not commercial." But disappointments were part of the game. I was to find that some of the better melodies were to get lost in the shuffle.

This all-American band got lost in the shuffle. The public stayed home and licked their financial wounds and listened to it, sweet and simple, on the radio from the Vallee-Lombardo school. The public would have none of us. Songs weren't selling and the frame in which I had visualized my puss hung high. Even Harry Hostetter, who had come on to New York, was in despair. "The

people won't listen," he says, "so jazz dies! Jazzbos walk
the street. Hot men sell apples. Steel down ten points.
Rails off. But never you mind, Hoagmichael, there'll
come a day." He went off brooding as my mind searched
for pleasanter things.

I recalled when Don Redman and McKinney's Cotton Pickers played the 1928 Prom. The unversity kids
had themselves a time. Don and his band really got a kick
out of watching the "finale hop," the most violent dance
they had discovered and a perfect expression for Don's
great music.

Also a fitting prelude for the Bent Eagles Book Nook
Commencement. When school was closing the Bent
Eagles, gathered from far and near for their burlesque
of the graduation exercises of the university. Wad Allen
—the out-of-town speaker—arrived complete with hen
and copy of his speech.

The exercises began with a parade, organized in East
Third Street, which proceeded to the Book Nook gathering crowds en route. Wad Allen, in a frock coat, top
hat, and with a white hen under his arm, led the parade.
He stood on a huge empty bus. Directly behind the bus
was a cornet jazz band led by the sardonic Semite who
dealt in secondhand clothes on the campus. He beat out
the rhythm with a yardstick and we of the band, clad in
bathrobes, came behind him.

Next came Eddie Wolfe, one of the newer and most
ardent contributors to the order, and Bill Moenkhaus.
They were symbolically arrayed in long black robes, to
which were attached huge white eagle wings. Their mode
of locomotion—a strange contraption swung between
large wobbly wheels—was drawn by a swayback white

horse, a horrible-looking creature. Pete Costas, the proprietor of the Book Nook, and a large following of Bent Eagles brought up the rear dressed in pajamas and bathrobes.

We filed into the Book Nook and found it jammed with students eager to hear the out-of-town speaker. Wad delivered his address from the balcony and the charter members of the Bent Eagles assisted Pete Costas in delivering diplomas to those of the student body who had spent most of their time in the Book Nook, during the school year, and showed other promise of holding aloft the mystic torch of the Bent Eagles.

Wad's speech was an inspiration to all. It was as insanely futile as a Bent Eagle's idea of posterity, as senseless as a Bent Eagle's idea of fame. Wad ad-libbed part of it and the speech is lost. I recall that it went something like this:

"Ya Lord and ya Lady Bent Eagles, friends, Foleys,[1] birds, and ya graduates; as the sheaves of years go passing by, comes this large class broken in mind and body seeking, through that limitless waste of years, those beautiful and intimate secrets known only to us Eagles.

Seated as I am, on a silver dollar, it seems that I should flap my wings. Some of you I do not know. There are others I do not know. In fact I am a total stranger.

Some of you will go away. There are others who will go away. Some of you will Sembower.[2] Perhaps this means that Cogshall[2] is not here. Leap, Cogshall, leap!

Ya Lord and ya Lady Bent Eagles, friends, Foleys,

---

[1] Ringer of the chimes.
[2] Local professors.

birds, and ya graduates, let me charge thee; I who from yon mountain comes to life; I from whom Mac Whore Ben Wilson. Let me charge thee three dollars.

As a concluding gesture Wad threw the flopping hen, mystic symbol of the true Bent Eagle, into the throng before him and the diplomas were then handed out.

Monk closed this solemn conclave, this session of spiritual rejuvenation in the value of the worthless, with an appropriate poem.

The Book Nook Commencement was one last gasp. A final despairing gesture of rebellion against the world of cold realities that was sweeping us into its grip.

Rebellion was dying in us, jazz was dying, too.

And I am back in New York and Monk is dead. Dead these months. The Old Man from Detroit came back to Bloomington and that doleful prophecy of his was fulfilled. "Any day now."

Monk never liked the scheme of things in this life, so he left it, and I believe his strange expressions were a form of protest. Perhaps jazz is a protest.

And then Bix. Five days now. *Little girl, why didn't you call me? Maybe a hospital, oxygen tent, little girl* . . .

He was walking to catch a train that would take him to a job, his horn under his arm, a somber fellow clad in a tuxedo, the raiment of his trade, a golden horn under his arm, walking toward a train, walking toward a bandstand; he collapsed. It was pneumonia. As simple and as quick as that. And she sent me his mouthpiece. A hunk of iron for a soul so sweet.

The "god-awful cokes," maybe they killed Monk. The god-awful music, maybe it killed Bix. The music that was in his mind, the music there was no expression for—beyond the beyond—and maybe he died on the upbeat. I remembered what he'd told me when I said I wouldn't quit music: "I won't either."

But he quit it, maybe on the upbeat, new things in his mind, new wonders to come from his horn. Maybe on the downbeat—but certainly happy, walking toward a bandstand, his horn under his arm.

The fraternity brothers—the "friends and sitters"—were scattered. Pink sent each of us a proclamation—a forerunner to a grand reunion:

Friends and Sitters!
Who'll deny that that magical year designated a long time ago as proper and fitting for solemn conclave has arrived?
We have rejoicing to do that each of us has survived these first perilous years. There must be swimming, rowing, walks in shady lanes, quoits, quarts and anagrams.
Brother Bell heads the committee on Arrangements, Arguments, Errands and Arrests.
I personally believe that Bloomington, in the early fall, while there is still faith in the football team and the water shortage has not set in, is the logical setting for the gathering. However, Brother Bell will gladly turn down any other suggestions you birds may have.
Cheerio!

The reunion was never held. Somehow they just never are.

❄

As tribute was, so now reversed it is
Then 'twas mine to give, and now 'tis his—

Monk wrote it and I quote it and somehow *Davenport Blues* comes to mind. Harry is there to lend encouragement, to say, "Go ahead, write that tune. What the hell do you care if it sounds screwy? It's right, isn't it? Remember what Reggie Duval said!"

But what's this they are saying? Up there on the shelf, under all that dust, Mills Music has a song called *Stardust*—Isham Jones has recorded it—a sellout. How come he recorded it? I wonder. Oh, yes, from Don to Jean to Vic to Jones. I remember now—a good play.

And I wonder if the song will be a hit. I sit by my phone in the musty office of an investment house hoping the publishers will call and tell me it is a hit. Afraid to call myself—afraid to ask.

The phone rings. I pick it up. It's Wad Allen.

"Bix died," he said.

And the tears came down my cheeks and I am laughing.

Editor's Note. *After reading the foregoing, Mr. Howard Allen, whom the reader will recall as Wad, felt impelled to write a letter to Hoagy Carmichael concerning the omissions, inadequacies and inconsistencies he felt were present in Hoagy's account of himself. Mr. Allen's letter is included here.*

Dear Hogwash McCorkle:

You are a very busy man. You do many things. You write music, you play music, you sing music, you direct music and maybe someday you'll even learn to read music —although none will believe me when I say that you can't. Anyway, what difference does it make now?

You learned at an early age to read books. But, as I looked over the manuscript for "The Stardust Road," I wondered why you went to the trouble to learn to read. That book was written by ear just as you write music. Reading certainly didn't teach you one of the "musts" in book writing—which is that you include all of the revealing details about your subject.

You happen to be the subject of this book, but at no place does it disclose what a worry you have always been to your friends for the reason that you've never learned to act like a spoiled celebrity. Also, it does not tell what a care you have been to us because every time you get interested in learning how to do something we always think you are going crazy before you master the problem. And it leaves out the fact that, each year since you arrived so successfully at the crest of "Star Dust Road," you have done a wide variety of such things as being a

radio star, becoming a popular and successful movie actor, and having two sons by only one wife.

To begin with, you certainly owe it to the public—
particularly to the youth of America, which can profit so
much from the example—to tell how your devotion to
the study and practice of law is the real, underlying cause
of your success in life. If it hadn't been for that, it
wouldn't have taken you years to get through Indiana
University. You would have missed a lot of good piano
practice, Carmichael; and at the same time you wouldn't
have acquired the faculty for deep and careful reasoning
which so often confounds us and which so often has led
you into dire straits. Yes, I remember, you *did* call the
turn of the big bear market to the day—that dreary July
day of 1932 but you sold too soon thereafter. And for that
we are happy because you might have struck it rich and
retired from song writing.

But you are lucky that way. You are lucky, aren't
you? Or did you have a deep reason why Bay View would
win the Santa Anita Handicap that day in the mud?
Thanks for the tip, old man; at fifty to one it came in
handy.

And may I say that in spite of the antidotes of legal
serum and the smoothing sirups administered by your
friends there were times when we feared you were a
goner. A typical warning of this, for instance, was the
time you had a sudden desire to learn to make drop
biscuits.

At one point in this, we decided to save you by getting your mind centered on golf. But, what happened
then? You became so completely obsessed by a mania for

golf, we had quickly to lure you back into the kitchen *but*—only to make Tom Collins' and like nobody else could. You always take a drink instead of letting it bother you.

You learned to play golf well. Sure, the same thing happened with tennis after you went to Hollywood. You made your greatest success as a composer by *not* writing songs about love. You gained popularity on radio and records by singing; yet you have no voice. How do you do that? It worries us. You got interested in movie acting about a year ago and now you are in that. Every time you put your mind to something you really get on the outside of it before you let go. That's the hell of it with you, Carmichael.

I know it was a heartbreaker when folks refused to let you practice law; they only wanted you to write music. And when you did give up the law practice you didn't even thank your friends and business associates for forcing you to become famous and make a lot of money. Instead, you had the feeling that the world had sold you short. So you walked through the rain in that Indianapolis park. You saw a little lonesome white flower there in the cold drizzle. You knelt in the wet grass beside the flower and talked to it. It was good-bye to all your past dreams and past ambitions. The next week you left for New York City.

And what happened then? *Stardust* was published (too bad) and that is where you wind up your book. I'm tired of reading about you, my friend, but don't you think maybe that was a mistake? Your wife, Ruth, and the two boys, Hoagy Bix and Randy Bob, and a lot of other things have come your way since the end of "Stardust Road."

To mention a few, you once again proved why you shouldn't be a lawyer by signing a contract with a publishing firm under which you came off second best. You wrote two hits, *Lazy River* and *Georgia on My Mind,* and carved my obituary on your apartment mantelpiece when I had such a bad hangover in your apartment that my hands wouldn't even shake. Then you put an up-and-coming boy named Johnny Mercer to work on some lyrics. Out came *Lazybones* which you two wrote in twenty minutes. Under the circumstances, you are not to be blamed for putting it into the works and forgetting about it.

Since you were still under the impression that music was a lousy business, we all put you on a boat headed for Europe where you made a two-bit tour in search of a new wealth of life. I don't know what happened over there that amounted to much, except you discovered that the youth of Europe was hungry for Jazz and you heard an orchestra in Budapest playing your tune, *March of the Hoodlums,* which you didn't even know had been published.

Then you caught a boat back and just before you landed in New York you listened to "Hit Parade" over the ship's radio. Much to your surprise and consternation, the number-one hit on that night's program was none other than *Lazybones,* which you had dashed off so hurriedly before you left, and then had proceeded to forget. When you got off the boat you found that *Lazybones* was a terrific hit, was selling 15,000 copies a day and was leading the way in helping to pull Tin-Pan Alley out of the depression. Not much, perhaps, but surely as important as the price you got for your college car, that dilapidated Open Job.

Then, too, you prided yourself on being quite a wolf, Carmichael, but you were soon to meet your match. It was not long after your return to these parts when a good-looking girl named Ruth Meinardi was introduced to you in your apartment. You plied her with her first drink of straight liquor and quickly got about your then customary business of being boldly progressive. No wonder she said you were crude, and no wonder I choked on my drink when she also said, "Nevertheless, I'm going to marry him someday." I'll say this for you, my friend. It took you quite a while to catch on and put your mind to this, but when you finally realized what a charming and talented girl you had, you really hit a crescendo with the gentle art of courtship.

It was one of the best things that could ever have happened to you. For Ruth wouldn't let you continue to lead a self-contained and one-track life. Ruth and her sister Helen, along with Sherman Fairchild and others, pulled you out of your shell, made you meet people—the New York set, the theater set. Jules Glaenzer was a helpful soul. And good old George Gershwin turned out to be one of the very best. Your night-clubbing shifted from strictly Harlem to more of the El Morocco type.

And you continued to demonstrate the agility for deep and careful reasoning which the study of law had brought to you. For instance, the manager of the Five Spirits of Rhythm asked you to help him start the first

Onyx Club. You turned him down. If you hadn't, of course, you would have cleaned up a small fortune.

You met Richard Rogers and he put you next to a job writing a Broadway show. As a result you produced the number called *Little Old Lady*, for "The Show Is On." All it did was turn out to be one of the most popular and biggest selling show songs in history. Pardon me for bringing up all these things, Carmichael, but if you are really trying to write a book about yourself, why did you leave them out?

Now, about that wedding. I suppose that somewhere during all this carrying on, you finally got around to making an honorable and orthodox proposal to Ruth. I couldn't swear to this. All I know is, you certainly approached the wedding in a most unusual fashion. First, Ruth left for London. Then you went to Barbados—you cabled Ruth to meet you there, so that you could both come back to New York together and get married. Since that was only three thousand miles out of her way, what you probably wanted her to do was help you cope with that "monkey" you had acquired. It tried to learn to drink like you do; instead, it just became a drunkard. And your cable to me announcing the wedding read like a calypso song—Winchell unscrambled it, however.

Fortunately your mother arrived from Indiana in company with your dad, "Cyclone" Carmichael, just in the nick of time. It was three days before the wedding and she had a few questions to ask. Had you made your arrangements at the church? Did you have your license? Had you sent invitations and completed the plans for the wedding reception to be held in your apartment? These and many others, to which most of your answers had to be "no."

Then she asked: "Hoagland, have you arranged for a best man?"

And you said: "Well, no. But I guess it will be Wad Allen."

And she said: "Don't you think it would be a good idea if you told *him* about it?"

You were married in the Fifth Avenue Presbyterian Church, where Ruth's father used to preach. McClelland Barclay, for whom Ruth often modeled, gave the bride away. And I forgot to pay the preacher. Remember?

Now about that fine hansom cab with the "just married" signs that conveyed the bride and groom to your East Fifty-second Street apartment: I *still* maintain we were not to blame because the horse tried to run away. Shame on you, Carmichael, for jumping to safety and leaving the bride in peril.

Thank goodness, George Gershwin was at the reception to lend it charm—he took your mother over to the piano, sat her down on the stool beside him, and asked her to play. She responded with *Maple Leaf Rag.* Then George played and sang all the leading tunes from "Porgy and Bess," a delightful preview of the light opera he had just written, and which was not to see the footlights for several months to come.

And you, as is so often the case, had neglected to put enough cash in your pocket. So we made up a pot and advanced the money to send the bride and groom upon their merry way to their wedding night, as Bunny Berrigan and his hot five cut loose with a Dixieland rendition of *Riverboat Shuffle*. All this made the front pages of the Sunday editions, so why not in your book?

Then you went to Hollywood to write *Small Fry, Two Sleepy People,* and *Heart and Soul* for Paramount Pictures. Just little nothings, I suppose. Then that eldest boy of yours, one Hoagy Bix, was born. This almost took place on the hospital steps due to your insistence that you takes movies of the whole blessed event. That one-track mind again.

That was almost as trying for us as was the night your second son, Randy Bob, was born. You will recall that this happened during the sixth ballot of the National Republican Convention in Philadelphia when they nominated our Hoosier friend, Wendell Willkie. You had your ears so plastered to the radio that you didn't hear the nurse tell you that you were the father of a fine baby son. Who could guess from all this that you were to become a better than average father? Honestly, Carmichael, we couldn't. But you are a strange man.

Many things happened. You telephoned me from Hollywood to learn if I knew who had written a certain poem which you had found scribbled on an old envelope —you had composed some music for it and were in a mess about publication. I said I didn't know who wrote the lyrics and advised you to tell Walter Winchell about it. You did and Winchell talked about it for three weeks on his broadcast. People from all over the United States claimed to be the author. You finally traced it down to a Mrs. Thompson in Philadelphia, who promptly died the night before Dick Powell introduced the song on the radio. The song, of course, was *I Get Along Without You Very Well*. Uninteresting, I suppose.

Ruth, in the meantime, was doing the same thing for you in Hollywood that she had done some years before in New York. Being attractive and personable, she had pushed you into the social swim. You bought a big Beverly Hills home, with swimming pool attached. You threw typical Hollywood parties with cellophane enclosures, tent over patio and pool. You and Ruth became good friends of people who influence others.

One of them influenced you to start a radio program for his company. What did Howard Hawks do for you? He decided you ought to be a motion-picture actor. And what did you do? You took it seriously. You played the part of Crickett in "To Have and Have Not" in support of Humphrey Bogart and Lauren Bacall. And you were a hit.

Since then you have done others: "Johnny Angel," "Canyon Passage," and now "The Best Years of Our Lives." You are rolling in dough. Does this mean that, after all these years, you haven't learned your lesson and that you still want to get out of the music business?

I suppose that your old playmates feel about you just the same as our mothers used to feel about us when we were taking part in a Children's Day entertainment at the church. They all sat in the front row and gave themselves ulcers worrying for fear we'd forget a line or start making faces at God.

So, to get right down to the point, I'll have to admit that your many friends not only get a thrill out of what you have done, but we also love to keep on feeling that you are an unpredictable, big-eared, dapper-looking guy about whom we'll have to keep on fretting for the rest of our lives. It should have been in the book.

Great world, ain't it, Hoagmichael?

So be it, so bend it and so burn it.

Wad Allen